Praise for Talking Change

"At last, a book that takes the challenging concepts of leading change and provides leaders with a practical tool to help them not only be more successful in navigating change, but to be more effective as leaders in general. There are hundreds of books on organizational change, but this one fully enables leaders to get down to the business of doing it, and doing it successfully."
Kallin L. Moore, MSc, EdD, Leadership and Organizational Effectiveness Consultant

"*Talking Change* is full of amazing knowledge and resources! While conversations through the different stages of change may feel daunting, uncomfortable or even impossible, Jen provides an amazing amount of tactical and practical advice as well as templates to help facilitate any conversation."
Candace Moody CPA, CA, Director, Master of Management, Haskayne School of Busines, University of Calgary

"This book is a must-read for anyone having conversations about change and/or wondering how to bring others on a change journey. Jen does an amazing job of cutting through the jargon and demystifying change management by incorporating personal stories, allowing the reader to have their own 'ah-ha' moments in connecting theory into practical daily application."
Anushka Tillakaratne, Senior Change Consultant, Canadian Tire Corporation Limited

"Most leaders intuitively know when a change conversation is necessary. Often though, the challenge is how do you a) start the conversation and b) structure the discussion to achieve the message/goal sought. *Talking Change* addresses these questions by providing leaders with an expert, yet highly practical, roadmap to essential change conversations. I have worked directly with Jennifer on change management initiatives and her book clearly articulates strategies we have successfully deployed to navigate change."
Jonathan, Legal Executive, Financial Services Firm

"In *Talking Change*, Jennifer Campbell presents a compelling and highly-practical guide for mastering the essential conversations shown to drive real and sustainable change. Filled with the who, what, why, when, and how of priming action, exploring impact, and generating positive momentum (AIM), Jennifer's expertise and refreshingly human approach is evident from the first page to the last."
Gabriella O'Rourke, Strategic and Operational Advisor, Morneau Shepell

"*Talking Change* is an insightful and practical guide in helping leaders have meaningful conversations towards driving change and overcoming resistance. Jennifer Campbell provides numerous tools, methodologies and illuminating stories that are a how-to for overcoming the challenges of getting the commitment to change and building consensus to delivering on that change."
Peter, Retired Partner, Professional Services Firm

"Jennifer Campbell's engaging new book *Talking Change* provides a complete range of well-considered 'plug and play' tools for change leaders that will motivate and sustain their people in moving through change transition gates. *Talking Change* belongs on every business leader's bookshelf — it's an essential go-to change management resource."
Linda N., Retired Chief Learning Officer, International Professional Services Firm

"This well-crafted, insightful book is the ultimate one-stop resource for anyone needing to manage change. Jennifer Campbell shares comprehensible steps that will spark optimal performance, team alignment, and a workforce dedicated to successful and shared results. Change is an unavoidable constant in today's environment and *Talking Change* is a blueprint to navigate it with positivity, commitment and success."
Cathy Goddard, Business Coach and Mentor Program Facilitator, Founder of Lighthouse Visionary Strategies, www.lighthousevisionary.com

"*Talking Change: Must-Have Conversations for Successful Leaders* is a must read! Campbell shares useful steps and resources business owners and managers need to move their organizations forward through thoughtful and well-planned dialogue. This is a book that I keep on my desk and refer back to constantly."
Caroline Bagnall, Founder, Connect Hospitality Strategies Inc., www.connecthospitality.ca

"Jennifer's message is timely as the world collectively tackles unprecedented changes affecting every human being. Especially when it comes to business, Jennifer's tactics on how to get people to buy into change, are straightforward and effective. Communication is the key to getting the commitment needed for effective change to take hold and Jennifer brings that message home."
Allison Gilchrist, Community Program Manager, Howe Sounds Women's Centre

"*Talking Change* is an excellent mix of practical tools and memorable stories and rhymes — all based on sound concepts and change management theory. Not only did I enjoy reading it through, I will also use it as a reference tool for years to come."
Rebecca Scott Rawn, Senior Director, Stakeholder Relations and Advocacy, Extendicare

"In *Talking Change*, Jennifer Campbell provides the appropriate mix of not only theory, but practical tips that can be utilized in our own journey through change. Her perspectives that using conversation to understand perspectives and ensure people feel heard is key to making real change last. This book is a practical tool that can be referenced each and every time we take on the challenge of change."
Paul C., Partner, Professional Services Firm

"*Talking Change* isn't just a business book, it's a practical guide for leaders to have more powerful and game changing conversations. Through easy to understand concepts, combined with storytelling, Jennifer Campbell provides you with a step-by-step blueprint to move yourself, your team, and your organization through change."
Theresa Lambert, Bestselling Author of *Achieve with Grace: A guide to elegance and effectiveness in intense workplaces*, Speaker, Professional Coach and Founder of Theresa Lambert Coaching & Consulting Inc. www.theresalambertcoaching.com

"Jen has written a must-read manual for managing change — which is now all of us, all the time. Her highly engaging book covers top level concepts of change and breaks them down into incredibly practical actions for those crucial change conversations. Jen's call to self-reflection is vital: people can be complicated, and change can be tricky, but we all benefit and grow when we successfully talk change."
Alison Macintyre, PhD. Consultant, Coach, Author, regenerem.com

"In *Talking Change*, Jennifer Campbell has done the heavy lifting for leaders needing to have conversations about change. She helps leaders know what conversations to have and when. Her practical templates guide leaders through the work they need to do to prepare for the difficult change conversations they need to have."
Jill Geddes, Founder, Trillium Teams

"*Talking Change* is exactly the book I need right now. It's a gold mine of practical tips and resources to hold the right conversations with the right people to address the huge amount of change happening in our industry."
Tory Kargl, Director, Whistler.com

"Upon reading *Talking Change*, one can tell that Jennifer Campbell is adroit on the topic of change and helping others deal with change. Jen was my leadership coach during the partnership process. Today, I am an equity partner and thriving with the team around me. This would not have been possible without Jen's direction on navigating many changes at once. After reading *Talking Change* I now have a playbook to reflect back on to help me deal with the ever-present challenge of change."
Ryan T., Partner, Professional Services Firm

"Jennifer has unlocked the tricky and magic box of change management in her new book. By curating and combining best-in-class thinking with her own deep hands-on experience, case studies, and tools she has created a one-stop-shop toolkit that will help you make change stick in your organization. This is essential reading for anyone who is embarking on a transformation journey."
Lori Sutej, Executive Coach, The Pivotal Point

Jennifer Campbell

TALKING CHANGE

Must-Have Conversations
for Successful Leaders

FALLON PUBLISHING

To Ellen and Evelyn

Two women who faced change with grace and determination and with whom I would still love to be in conversation.

Contents

Action Impact Movement

Commit to Action. Make an Impact. Create the Movement.

ACTION IMPACT MOVEMENT (AIM) partners with organizations to build leadership depth and implement change that sticks. We **coach people** to become resilient, change-savvy leaders who adapt, innovate, and inspire their teams and organizations to realize results. We **facilitate conversations** to improve team dynamics, and engage and align teams around common goals, behaviors, and expectations. We **create structure, process, and habits** to sustain success.

Are you ready to take AIM? Let's connect.

jen@actionimpactmovement.com
www.actionimpactmovement.com
in, Jennifer Campbell

How to Use This Book

Talking Change focuses on conversations. More specifically, what I call *AIM Changing Conversations*. These must-have conversations help you lead change successfully. And if you're a leader in today's organizations, chances are you lead change. These conversations inspired the name of my company — **Action Impact Movement**. When you get these conversations right you will gain commitment to **Action**, make an **Impact**, and create **Movement** toward desired results.

In Part One I explain the foundations of change and why it's often challenging. In Part Two I discuss *why* and *how* to have conversations and with *whom*. Finally, in Part Three, I provide the structure and questions for *20 AIM Changing Conversations* that you can use in different situations to lead change that sticks.

If you can relate to one or more of the following scenarios, you're in the right place! You are:

- Seeking new ideas and new tools to manage resistance to change, gain commitment, and motivate people to do things differently in your team or organization.

- Leading a new team and want to make changes to people, processes, or outcomes.
- Starting from scratch with a new initiative and want to get it right the first time.
- Half-way through a major change and need to get it back on track.
- Keen to accelerate the pace of change to realize the benefits as soon as possible.
- A leader who wants to build their capability to embrace change and lead better!

Read in a weekend. Reference for a lifetime.

You can read this book from cover-to-cover to get the full picture of what to expect when leading change, identify potential roadblocks, and learn how to facilitate conversations with confidence. Or you can use this book as a convenient reference, for example:

- Flip to the conversation you need to have right now and use the conversation planner to prepare for it.
- Review the reasons for resistance to change and identify what you can do to address it.
- Assess where your team is on the ABC Transition Roadmap™ and make a plan to gain their commitment to change.
- Use the Self-Reflection Conversations to assess your own reactions and path forward during change.

Write notes, add your own questions, or combine two or more conversations. Whether you enjoy facilitating and participating in conversations or not, *Talking Change: Must-Have Conversations for Successful Leaders* will prepare you to lead change that sticks. Let's start Talking Change!

One More Time with Feeling

CONVERSATIONS CREATE DEBATE, understanding, agreement, and the impetus needed to move people and organizations to embrace change. Each conversation is important. Each one a catalyst for change, no matter how small. The same conversation will be had multiple times, with the same or different people, in order to build momentum. Hence the need to have conversations — *one more time with feeling!* — to move people to commit and continue on the path toward change.

I love being in conversation, it's my extraverted preference. Conversation is how I learn, how I gather ideas, digest information, and make decisions. Some of those conversations are with myself. Many of those conversations are with others — friends, family, co-workers, mentors, or strangers I meet on the ski lift. Each conversation adds new information to my life and impacts my thinking and actions. I've facilitated thousands of conversations over the years — from one-on-one to large group settings — with the purpose of moving not only myself, but other people and organizations, to a new and better state.

Change requires persistence. The road to revitalization, revision, and transformation is not a straight one. There are stops and starts, and sideways shuffles, two steps forward and one step back. The fact is, all of these movements are driven by conversations.

Conversation has been the lens through which I have looked at all my materials, research, and experiences related to leading change. I gained my foundation for leading change early in my career. In the years since then I have cemented not only my passion for supporting and enabling change in people and organizations, but also my knowledge in how to make it happen. The pieces have fallen into place and over the years my experience in applying theory has led me to create practical steps to help others lead and thrive through change.

In this book I will talk about why conversations are needed to enable change in organizations, what conversations will help people pivot, who needs to be included in conversations, and how to facilitate the conversations that will move people from the old world to the new world (and through the messy in-between phase). You will learn the must-have conversations to lead change successfully — the conversations to plan and manage change and to engage employees in the change process. You'll also learn what conversations you need to have with yourself to uncover your approach when faced with change. I'll provide simple tactics that work and demystify the world of leading change based on my years of experience from the board room to the plant floor. You will gain the confidence to lead AIM Changing Conversations every day, no matter what change comes your way.

Through your conversations you will uncover resistance to change, identify new solutions, and create movement towards your end goal. Naturally, people will ask, dissent, disagree, and debate, yet hopefully keep an open mind to different perspectives. Healthy disagreement opens up new conversation paths. So don't shy away from it.

"

There is no conversation more boring than the one where everybody agrees.
Michel de Montaigne

You will have conversations — *one more time with feeling* — looking at topics from different points of view and bringing new ideas to the discussion. It may feel like you are going in circles, and you might be, until one conversation clicks, and you finally find the off-ramp.

Think of something you have aimed to change. How many times have you had the conversation?

One of my daughters resists going to ski school every Saturday. Yet, every Saturday afternoon at pick up she talks non-stop about the things she did, how terrified she was on the edge of a cliff, and how she dropped in anyway. She is proud of her accomplishments. Yet, come the next Saturday we have the same conversation about not wanting to go!

I engage in the conversation most Saturdays, reminding her of the fun she will have, of how happy and proud she is every time after lessons — *one more time with feeling*. On the days I don't engage in the conversation and simply give up, allowing her to fall back into her comfort zone of staying home, no one is happy — I miss my day of skiing, she doesn't get enough exercise or social interaction, and we move backwards, not forwards.

Don't get discouraged. Be supportive. Have the conversation — *one more time with feeling* — to move forward. It's not easy to get people to buy into change, let alone stay changed, but seeing how happy they can be once they have accepted a new perspective or accomplished something they didn't think was possible is a great reward.

Transitioning to something new is often a long-term commitment that needs to be taken one day at a time, one conversation at time. My sister climbed Mount Kilimanjaro years ago. She said it was one of the hardest things she has ever done — mentally and physically. Her approach was 'one foot in front of the other', just focus on the next step. Slowly but surely, she made it to the top and the reward was priceless.

So is the nature of change. One conversation at time. Seemingly the same conversation over and over — *one more time with feeling*. Conversations will drive actions. Actions will drive change.

Whether you are new to leading change, accountable for implementing change in a team, a change practitioner, a project manager, a people manager, or a sponsor of change, you can refer to this book for ideas on how to craft change-inducing conversations. Leading change has become a core competency of any leader. This book, with a bit of theory and a lot of practical tools, will help you successfully lead people and organizations through constant change.

Change is changing.

No longer is change a one-time-only event with a beginning and an end, but a continuous journey to adapt to customer expectations, competitive innovation, environmental evolution, and technological disruption. The new normal is constant change. Doing it faster and better than your competition and gaining people's commitment to do something more, better, or different are the keys to success. Commitment is gained when people feel heard. People feel heard when they are engaged in conversation.

Let the AIM Changing Conversations begin!

Chapter Summaries and Rhymes

I'm known for saying, "one more time with feeling." There are a lot of repetitive actions and conversations when leading change and it can be hard to stay motivated to do the same things over and over again. *One more time with feeling* became my saying to recognize that change is hard, but we need to keep going. I use this phrase for chapter summaries throughout the book.

I'm also known for creating rhymes. It stems from my mom suggesting I deliver my grade four speech in rhyme format for an interesting twist. Since then I've used rhymes to celebrate colleagues' careers, summarize projects, crystallize key points in a memorable way, and to add a bit of levity when the going gets tough. Here's the first rhyme in the book.

I started my career in a consulting firm, working long hours and keen to learn,

We had clients who needed our help to make change, acquire and merge, and get their teams more engaged,

So I joined the change team, intrigued by the goal to move people to adopt a new system or role,

Our quest was to enable, change can't simply be managed, as people must believe the change is to their advantage,

I implemented, re-engineered and created flow charts; teaching change to new hires was my favorite part,

Over the years I gained great experience and skill, had success and some failures, pushed water uphill,

My models, my ideas, my tips, tools and tricks, line these pages for those who wish to lead change that sticks,

TALKING CHANGE

Learn how to hold conversations to move people to action; make an impact, create the movement, and gain the right traction,

To lead yourself and lead others through change, which is truly a constant in this day and age!

Being a Successful Leader During Change

" ▬▬▬▬
A great change leader creates other change leaders.
John Kotter

If you are a leader in today's organizations, you lead change.

The role of the leader during change cannot be underestimated. I'll define leaders in several ways. They are those who lead and manage others in an organization. They are the face of the organization to the outside world with customers, suppliers, regulators, media, partners, or others. They are the pilot teams during change rollouts. They are the people who are expected to have answers. They are the ones who need to build movement and momentum towards the new desired state. They may not have been the ones who decided on the change, but they are accountable to drive the adoption of the change in their teams to transform the organization. They are the first to be asked questions, the target of others' frustration, and the ones to make tough decisions about people and processes. They have to lead through the unknown.

How you handle the unknown will define your leadership ability.

Leading in the grey space, as I like to call it, means leading when things are uncertain and forging ahead regardless. It is the place where true leaders are made and herein lies the need to facilitate conversations: to ask, to listen, and to decide on action.

As a leader, you won't know all the answers to all the issues that will arise, or all the questions that may be asked. Let's be honest, we would never change if we waited until we had all the answers first. Yes, the timelines will be delayed, the product will not be finished, the people will not jump on board the minute you ask them to. But to lead through the grey space is to bring your people along with you and come out the other side having navigated change successfully.

Leading change, like running a marathon, takes endurance. As my colleague Leslie Keen so aptly wrote in her article *Is outstanding change leadership more passion than process?* (Leslie Keen and Graham Stephenson, 2009): "Leaders need to stay the course, with time and other business priorities as the enemy. Endurance is vital for the survival and development of any worthwhile change effort. Only a team that develops the necessary endurance — supported and encouraged by the leader — will be able to withstand the stress, frustration, uncertainty and ambiguity which often accompanies major change."

And just as you determine the right running pace during a marathon, as a leader you need to establish an optimal pace of change for not only moving your organization forward but also to enable the absorption of change by your people. Too much change at once will paralyze people, too little change will not produce the desired transformation. There is no magic to the 'right amount of change', engaging in conversations will help determine how much, how fast, and how often change can be assimilated successfully into your organization.

Your Role as a Leader During Change

As a leader during change you will:

- Not have all the answers
- Not always agree with the direction
- Not always know all the details of what's happening with the change
- Not always have your team members on side and 'rowing in the same direction'
- Not always have extra time in your day to 'deal with the change'

So, what will you have as a leader during change?

- The chance to make an impact on your team and organization
- The chance to take calculated risks for greater rewards
- The chance to try new things
- The chance to engage in conversations to listen, learn, and influence
- The chance to inspire
- The chance to lead

One More Time with Feeling

Leading through change is a big undertaking,

Navigating transition, resistance and making,

Decisions when not all the answers are known,

During the ending, exploring and new beginning zones,

Success will be yours as a leader of change,

With patience and practice to use the full range,

Of conversations to plan, engage, and reflect,

Take the lead, you'll be great, it's time to affect,

Yourself and your people to realize improvement,

Take action, make an impact, create the movement,

That drives our world forward to change and transform,

You've got this, I know you'll step up and perform,

So lead with your questions to bring others in,

Together you'll create the right solutions to win!

PART ONE

What Happens During Change

Change Definitions

1

CHANGE IS OFTEN a reaction to external forces such as technological advancements, customer feedback, competition, new regulations, mergers and acquisitions, privatization, and local, national, or global events. We've all been through many changes in our lives; at home, at work, and beyond. To set the stage for AIM Changing Conversations, let's examine what happens when change is introduced in an organization; this will give us a better idea of why conversations are needed to realize success.

What is Change?

Change happens around us all the time. Today we use system X, in two months we will use system Y. Today my team includes five people focused on sales, next week my team will have twelve people focused on sales and service. Today it takes 10,000 loyalty points to buy $10 worth of groceries, next week it will take 12,000 points.

The change is what is going to be different.

Change is the event that takes place. Switching on a new system. Hiring a new leader. Implementing a new expense policy. Or introducing a new technology platform to enable an entire workforce to work remotely. Change is undertaken to realize different results, for example, more revenue, more efficiency, more opportunities, or to comply with new regulations.

Project management offices around the globe have mastered the science of change, of moving from X to Y, of organizing, project planning, Gantt charting, and status reporting the actions it will take to migrate to a new state.

So, why are 'change management' roles becoming more prevalent? Why do I regularly get phone calls from leaders desperate not to repeat the failures of the past or hoping that the change can happen faster this time so as to capitalize on the immediate market opportunity? Because of people. Because of feelings. Because people react to and interpret change differently. Because people transition through change, from the old world to the new world, at different paces.

Consider the example of a business that leases a substantial amount of office space. A surge in market demand for similar space drives up rent. In response, the business decides to reduce its office footprint to decrease costs. The reduction in office space is the change, the decreased costs are the desired result. However, the reduction in office space means people who used to have their own offices are now forced to share space. This may lead to benefits, like increased collaboration, or challenges, like interpersonal conflict. Making the change to the office footprint is the easy part; navigating the transition from one way of working to another is where the real work begins. So, where change can be relatively quick, transition takes time, patience, and yes, conversation!

What is Transition?

"
It isn't the changes that do you in, it's the transitions.
William Bridges

Transition is the experience of moving the hearts and minds of people to adopt a new future state. It is a personal internal process. American Author William Bridges describes transitions as "the inner psychological process that people go through as they internalize and come to terms with the new situation that the change brings about" (*Managing Transitions*, 1991). This definition has stood the test of time — it's still the same process for people today. Bridges goes on to describe the three stages of transitions: endings, neutral zone, and beginnings.

ENDINGS – the process of understanding what is going to be different and letting go of the current state.

NEUTRAL ZONE (EXPLORING) – the process of dealing with potential losses, recognizing and addressing resistance, trying out new ways of doing things. This is a stage of exploring.

BEGINNINGS – the process of choosing new behavior and attitudes, accepting a new way of doing things and gaining the benefits of the change.

Think of moving to a new house. The actual change is quite straightforward; you sell the old house, take possession of the new house and move in. The transition however takes more time. Endings create feelings of loss — friends left behind in your old neighborhood, the garden you loved in the backyard, your custom dining table that won't fit in your new house.

And even though you may be moving to a bigger, better house in a more 'desirable' neighborhood, you still have to reconcile your feelings of leaving something behind to move to something new. You enter the exploring zone, as you unpack in the new house, meet friendly neighbors, and find a new coffee shop. Something begins as you start to accept the change and adopt a new lifestyle. You even stop opening the wrong cupboard for the plates (because in your old house they were next to the sink and this muscle memory continued for a while). You now appreciate that your walk to the transit system is shorter and less windy. You have fond memories of the old house, but they are being overtaken by experiences in the new house. And while your purchase contract committed you to the new house weeks or months before, your heart and mind have finally committed to your new home.

What do we know about personal transitions during change?

1. Each individual has a unique capacity to change based on experience, personality, and circumstances

2. Change creates uncertainty

3. Change means dealing with emotions and feelings

4. Change requires energy – more brain power to learn new systems or processes, more physical energy to do the same work in a new way

5. Change requires risk – more mistakes are made with the potential to look foolish in front of others, or the possible negative impact on current or long-term career options

6. Change requires time to adjust – transition happens on a different timeline than the actual change

7. Change taxes capacity – introducing multiple changes strains people's ability to absorb and assimilate change, especially when it is introduced quickly

You cannot develop a new identity or sense of purpose until you have let go of the old one.

This hit me in the face (almost literally) recently. I knocked my teeth out when I was nine, jumping on a pogo stick in my friend's garage. We were seeing how many times we could spring up and down on the pogo stick without stopping. My competitive nature got the better of me and, as I sailed past my friend's high score, the rubber stopper on the end of the metal pipe gave way. Metal on smooth concrete is not a good combination. I ended up falling face down, hard, on the cement, and breaking my two front teeth. Thus began a years-long saga of fake front teeth.

While in university I ended my bi-yearly teeth switch by having a permanent bridge affixed. I was told it would last twenty years! In those twenty years I graduated university, met and married my husband, made new friends across the country, and established my career. I was known for my 'million dollar' smile (which is probably about how much my parents felt they paid in dental bills). In every smiling picture my teeth are showing; everyone I know only remembers me with those teeth.

A few years back I started to explore the possibility of what's next, what will happen when I finally need to replace this bridge, which is now well past its 'best before date'. I went to a well-regarded dental surgeon and was in tears by the end of the appointment. She had presented all the things she could do, told me how much better my teeth would be, and explained how much better they would look.

So why was I in tears if she was going to make everything better? Because she didn't ask me any questions but rather told me *her* answer to *my* problem. I felt she had no respect for my past, no respect for my current teeth, no regard for how much those teeth meant to me — they were part of who I was — my story, my smile. Her assessment, based on my teary reaction, was that I was not a good candidate for the next step. Full stop. No helping me through the transition, no thought about what I might lose by replacing those teeth. She had a vision for what my new smile could be, but I wasn't even close to buying in, let alone believing in the need for it or the viability of it. That was the end of that.

I didn't need to replace the bridge right away, so the next time I was visiting a jaw specialist (my jaw joints are another casualty of the pogo stick incident), who also performs tooth implants and bridge work, I asked for his opinion. And what a different style! He asked me questions, engaged me in conversation, and listened to my answers.

I haven't gone ahead with the change yet. I will. But to move through endings successfully we need to respect the past and recognize that it was the best decision or best action at the time, and also that it's done, you cannot change the past. To start a new chapter, we must accept that it's time to let go of the past, of past identities, attitudes, behaviors, or artifacts, and start the transition to move to a new beginning. And this transition requires conversations, to feel heard, to change perspectives, and to finally move on.

What influences the rate at which people reach the Beginnings stage?

1. **ROLE IN THE CHANGE** – those who planned or instigated the change will transition first

2. **EXTENT OF IMPACT OF THE CHANGE** – the change will affect people and functions differently, the extent of the change will impact their transition rate

3. **PERSONALITY TYPE** – different personality types and different style preferences react differently to change

Transitioning at different rates is like running a marathon. Those that are leading the change finish the marathon long before those just learning about the change. It's important for the leaders to remember what it was like to start the race — tying shoe laces, warming up, the mass of people crossing the starting line before being able to find your own space to run. Leaders need to go back and bring people along the racecourse with them, engage them in conversation, find out how they are doing and what they are

> When some have already run the races, others are still doing up their laces.

feeling. Where a cramp or dehydration can negatively impact your desired race results, lack of transition support can negatively impact the desired benefits of an organizational change.

As with marathon running, if you're exhausted and sore in the middle of the run, it may seem like a mistake to have started; the middle of change may also have you wondering why you started in the first place. I worked with an organization where a dysfunctional leader was removed. For a period of time the team was relieved, and the stress levels were lowered, however, before a new leader was hired the team started to wish the previous leader was back. They were growing weary of their extra responsibilities in the absence of a leader and the mood that had been lightened was now being clouded again by inter-team squabbles. They logically knew that the return of the previous leader was not the right answer but in the middle of a change it's natural to start thinking the original situation was not all that bad. Stay the course, be resilient. Go back to *why* the change is being made and use that compelling reason as a beacon through the tough times.

What is the impact of transition on organizations?

During the transition — between the ending of one event and before the full start of the next one — is often when people are less productive, less focused, or leave organizations. They become disillusioned, frustrated, demotivated, confused, and feel like they can't get their bearings. A friend worked for a progressive organization, she led the IT team and implemented cutting-edge systems and solved technology issues as soon as they arose. Her organization was bought by a giant player in the market with multiple branches and sites. Although her company had better systems and processes, they were now but one small player in the larger scene. Their technology systems were discontinued and they had to adopt and implement the less-sophisticated IT systems of their new parent organization. They encountered many issues and she and her team couldn't solve problems the way they used to. For two years she continued to try to make it work until finally she'd had enough and left for a new opportunity.

This story demonstrates that the 'messy middle' of the neutral zone can go on for many months and years. That is a long time to have people living in uncertainty and feeling the stress that comes in the midst of transition. This is a large risk to organizations: the threat of people leaving and people not producing their best work due to frustration and confusion. Hence the paramount need to effectively enable transitions. And, these transitions are enabled through conversations.

Conversation is an irreplaceable tool to help people transition through change. Whereas project management focuses on change at the organizational level, conversation is a way to motivate change at the individual level and support people through transitions. Do you feel more compelled to change when you receive a mass email setting out your deadlines for implementing the change, or when a colleague takes you out for a one-on-one coffee and explains the rationale for the change? *Going beyond traditional project management plans to include transition plans is the starting point for change management.*

My messy middle story

I left my first 'real' job, a consulting role, to join an organization as a project manager. Making the decision to leave the consulting firm was challenging but I got over my hesitations and joined the new organization. It started well, people were nice, I was invited to interesting meetings, people were keen to hear my views from my previous experience. I was on a roll, and then I wasn't... I had hit the middle of the neutral zone, the messy middle. I doubted my choice to leave my old world, I doubted my skills, I didn't feel supported (because I wasn't asking for help), I was starting to spiral into confusion. This was a personal change that I had chosen and here I was not quite fully committed to the change. I felt like I was swimming against the tide. I was at work late one night rewriting a project charter for the fifth time and becoming paralyzed with frustration. I was clinging to my past identity, the success I'd had in my previous organization, but it was no longer serving me, I needed help and had to accept that.

I initiated a conversation with my leader, admitting that I needed help. I explained my frustrations and to my surprise he wasn't surprised. He expected that I would need help, he knew the project wasn't going to be straight-forward, he wasn't expecting it to be done by the tight deadline I had given myself. What a relief. And what good lessons to learn: in order for something new to truly begin (embrace my new role in a new company), I had to (1) bring forward the useful skills from my past but let go of my previous identity, (2) engage in multiple conversations to learn, gain perspective, and consider next steps, and (3) commit to being in a new role and making decisions aligned with the direction of my new organization. The conversation with my leader helped me feel like I had a chance of getting through the transition to succeed in my new role. And I did.

What is Change Management?

The last term we'll discuss is change management. Change management is a growing field of study and work. It involves strategies and activities to help an organization realize its desired outcomes from a change. A successful change initiative includes both project management *and* transition plans. Project management activities, including a project charter, scope documents and plans that address timelines, budget, project resourcing, and decision making, are generally focused on the three phases of a change:

- **PREPARE**: identifying the desired change, reviewing the business processes and organizational structures impacted, developing requirements for technology or other tools, planning go-live dates, and assessing the environment to determine a path forward.

- **IMPLEMENT**: accomplishing tasks needed to move from the old to the new (e.g., ordering new hardware, developing new organization charts, hiring people).

- **EVALUATE**: measuring the results of the change — were the benefits realized, what adjustments need to be made, etc.

Transition plans focus on the strategies and activities to support people through the three phases of transition (endings, exploring, and beginnings), enabling them to commit to and continue working in the new way. Organizations engage in many different tactics to support personal transitions including: readiness assessments, communication, training, aligning performance measures to new behaviors, coaching, visible sponsorship, and yes, conversations.

Change management is the combination of successfully working through the three phases of change (prepare, implement, evaluate) and the three phases of transition (ending, exploring, beginning) in parallel, to enhance the chances for success and realize the desired benefits of the change. Most organizations have felt the pain of great financial, time, and human expense to make a change, without realizing the benefits. And in doing so, they have compromised future change efforts. People lose faith in leadership's ability to implement change and are hesitant to go through the experience again. The practice of change management is especially needed when:

The change is major:

- It affects a significant portion of operations or business units
- It affects core operations

There is a high cost of implementation failure:

- Disruption of operations
- Disruption to the customer experience

There is a high risk that the lack of successful personal transitions could result in:

- Failure to adopt new technology, processes, or behaviors
- Sabotage

Achieving desired business results from change requires follow through on both project plans *and* transition plans.

Let's say your organization is implementing training to improve the sales skills of your customer-facing employees. The business goals are to build stronger relationships and increase sales revenue. The project of providing training may be deemed a success — the right vendor was identified, all employees attended the training, participants provided rave reviews about the training. However, the lack of transition may hinder the overall business success.

The old way of selling may no longer exist (you removed the old training content and tools), but people have gotten 'stuck' in the transition between ending and beginning. People attended the training, but they are not getting coached or supported to use new skills. They don't understand *why* they had to change when they believed they were selling effectively before. They have forgotten what they learned at training so are not using the new language or forms correctly. If people don't apply their new skills successfully, the investment in the sales training is not realized, money and time are wasted, and the future state of increased revenue won't come to pass. Hence the need to not only plan and manage change but to also enable the people side of change — to help people through transition using a series of actions and engaging in conversations to change behavior and performance, and realize the desired business outcomes.

AIM Changing Conversations to Enable Transitions

While I have many resources and have taught many courses on the practice of change management, our focus in this book is to enable transition — moving people from endings to beginnings to commit to and continue the change — through conversation.

I recently saw Hayley Wickenheiser, a Canadian Olympic hockey champion, speak at a conference. She left the crowd with three takeaways:

1. Pressure is a privilege — make the most of it

2. Control what you can, let go of what you can't

3. Adapt or die — be open to change

As a leader accountable for transitioning people through change — to adopt a new system, structure, process or something else — you are pressured to produce results, and although you may not have control over what is changing, you can choose to personally adapt and motivate your team to adapt for greater success. AIM Changing Conversations will help you do just that.

One More Time with Feeling

CHANGE – what is actually going to be different (e.g., new system, new team members, new structure, new processes).

TRANSITION – the personal internal process people go through to acknowledge and accept the change in order to embrace the new state (from endings, through the exploring zone, to new beginnings).

CHANGE MANAGEMENT – the combination of successfully working through the three phases of change (prepare, implement, evaluate) and the three phases of transition (ending, exploring, beginning) in parallel, to enhance the chances for success and realize the desired benefits of the change.

CAPACITY FOR CHANGE – each individual has a unique capacity to change based on experience, personality, and circumstances.

RATE OF TRANSITION – people will reach the beginning stage of change at different rates based on their:

- **Role in the change:** those who planned the change will transition first
- **Extent of impact of the change:** how they are affected by the change
- **Personality type:** different personalities embrace change at different rates

Change is managed with milestones and charts. Using plans to track status and monitoring each part,

Transition is facilitated to win hearts and minds. Through conversations we believe, we commit, and align,

To the opportunities and results the change will address. Then move to a new normal to create greater success.

The ABC Transition Roadmap™

2

NOW THAT WE have reviewed some key change definitions, we'll look at how people react to change and how to help them move through transition. **Individuals need to change in order for the organization to be changed.** The ultimate destination is to influence people to commit to and continue doing something more, better or different in pursuit of the desired business results. Let's see what happens when change is announced.

The Seven Dynamics of Change

One of the activities I often use when leading training sessions reveals the Seven Dynamics of Change. American Author Ken Blanchard wrote about the predictable patterns that people go through when experiencing change, regardless of whether it's chosen or imposed.

During change, people:

1. Feel awkward and uncomfortable

2. Focus on what they have to give up

3. Feel all alone

4. Can only take so much change

5. Have different levels of readiness

6. Are concerned about not enough resources

7. Revert back the old way of doing things if not pressured to stay changed

Let's dive a little deeper into what these mean:

1. **AWKWARD AND UNCOMFORTABLE**: change breeds uncertainty and uncertainty makes people feel uncomfortable. Think of going to a party with people you don't know. There are some awkward and uncomfortable moments as you aim to break into conversations with others, it takes some time before you find common ground or meet people you may want to chat with. Sometimes this dynamic presents itself as people trying to look their best. In organizations, this may mean people clean up their offices or raise their hand more in meetings — they are not sure what is coming so they put their best foot forward; but, of course, it can be done in an awkward fashion since they are not quite sure what 'best foot' they need to put forward in order to accommodate and accept this change. Consider the first time you went to the grocery store during the COVID-19 pandemic; it was awkward and uncomfortable as people tried to stay apart and not touch too many things on their way to the checkout line.

2. **FOCUS ON GIVE UPS**: the first phase in transition is endings. Something has to end before something else can begin. Thus, people feel like they are going to lose something during a change, even if it's something they didn't like in the first place! People usually focus on what they will lose before they focus on what they may gain. Transition is a personal experience — so even though the gain is better for the organization, what a person personally loses is where they focus first. For example, a school implemented a new volunteer sign-in process to ensure the safety of the children — child safety sounds like a great goal. However, the new process meant volunteers had to stop at the office upon entry and wear a bright blue badge around the halls. Volunteers initially focused on what they felt they had lost — their freedom

to move about the school as they wished, before recognizing the value of what was being gained — the increased safety of their children. And they felt awkward and uncomfortable sporting their bright blue badge!

3. **FEEL ALONE**: change can create anxiety and can make people feel vulnerable. Therefore, during change they may isolate themselves to avoid showing their feelings to others. My parents divorced when I was a teenager. I have two siblings so we were all going through the same thing at the same time, but instead of relying on each other, we all felt as though we were managing the change alone. This same thing occurs in organizations. Many people go through change at the same time but feel as though they are going through it alone and that their situation is unique. People don't ask questions for fear of looking foolish, therefore, they get frustrated trying to figure out new systems or processes on their own. They may believe that they are the only one struggling when it's more likely that many people are having similar challenges due to the change.

4. **CAN ONLY TAKE SO MUCH CHANGE**: it is a rare occurrence that one change is completely finished before a new one begins. They may seem like different changes — a new technology versus a business unit restructure, but when the same people are impacted by all of these changes, weariness and change fatigue set in. I managed a team who developed training programs. One month we received three different requests to make changes to the programs. One group was implementing a new evaluation system so all the evaluations had to be changed in the programs. Another group implemented a new learning management system and all the programs had to be renamed and reorganized. A third group upgraded the technology platform many of the programs were built in, so those programs had to be upgraded as well. Each of these groups had only one change they were focused on, but *all* their changes landed on the training development team at the same time. One of those changes would have been manageable alongside the development team's day jobs, but three in one month

was too much and change fatigue set in. To move forward we delayed some of the changes and, where possible, found others to assist to decrease the workload and still make the changes happen.

5. **DIFFERENT LEVELS OF READINESS**: some people will be enthusiastic about the change right away but then their interest may dwindle as the change drags on. Others may take a bit longer to prepare themselves for the change, but then they'll finally convert. What is often true is that the longer a change takes, the less enthusiasm everyone has for continuing the change with no end in sight. A team I worked with migrated to a new online collaboration platform. Some team members jumped on board right away, posted ideas and helpful tips, and booked all their meetings in this new platform. Other team members, however, continued to use the old platform until it was decommissioned before finally switching over. Different levels of readiness may be due to fear of the unknown and trying to stay in the current state for as long as possible. Or, it may be due to perceived lack of time or ability to learn the new way. It can also be due to different personality traits — some personalities are more likely to adopt change faster than others (more on this in Chapter Seven).

6. **NOT ENOUGH RESOURCES**: executing a change is usually something you have to do on top of your 'day job', therefore people often don't feel as though they have enough time, money, resources, equipment, or energy to make the change. Until they have the chance to stop doing something else, they feel stretched in too many directions. For example, I worked with a team that was implementing a new methodology. The training was extensive, and more work was required under the new methodology. The team was under pressure to make the switch without missing client deadlines. I helped the team identify activities they could delay, delegate to other groups, or simply stop doing. This freed up time and money to focus on the methodology change and meet client deadlines.

7. **REVERT BACK TO THE OLD WAY**: I've belonged to various fitness gyms in my life and every January there is an influx of people in the classes. This lasts about a month, maybe two, before the numbers level out again because the 'new year's resolutioners' have quit the gym. People need a reason to stay changed. If you are not seeing the results you want in the time you wanted to see them, your motivation wanes. The present state is comfortable, and in order to move out of that comfort zone, there needs to be a really good reason. Each person's reason will be different to not only try something new, but to embrace and continue in the new way. The reason for changing needs to be stronger than the reason for staying the same. And, reinforcement is needed to continue in the new state.

The following chart outlines elements of a successful transition mapped against the Seven Dynamics of Change. The next section gives you ideas on how to navigate them successfully. Here's a hint: it involves conversations!

DYNAMICS OF CHANGE	SUCCESSFUL TRANSITION REQUIRES
1. Awkward and uncomfortable	Voicing discomfort and someone going first to demonstrate the new way, enabling others to feel comfortable following
2. Focus on losses vs gains	Letting go of actions or identities that don't serve the future
3. Feel all alone	Collaborating to solve challenges and celebrating success together
4. Can only take so much change	Support to prioritize work and build resilience
5. Different levels of readiness	The opportunity to discuss concerns, ideas, and next steps
6. Not enough resources	Making choices and decisions about priorities
7. Revert back to normal	A compelling reason and reinforcement to stay changed

Navigating the Seven Dynamics of Change

The Seven Dynamics of Change reminds me of the movie *Elf* (2003), where Buddy the Elf talks about his journey from the North Pole to New York City: "I passed through the seven levels of the candy cane forest, through the sea of swirly-twirly gum drops, and then I walked through the Lincoln Tunnel." Transition can feel like this swirly-twirly journey. Buddy was leaving Santa and his elf family behind (his ending) to find his new life with his dad's family in New York (his beginning). His journey to get to New York City and the rest of the movie demonstrate his successful, yet bumpy, transition to finding his own place in the world.

How do leaders navigate the Seven Dynamics of Change beyond the world of elves and candy? And how do they achieve what a successful transition requires? Through AIM Changing Conversations; specific conversations to guide people through the transition; from endings, to exploring, to new, successful beginnings. And how do leaders know what conversations to have and when? They follow the ABC Transition Roadmap™.

The ABC Transition Roadmap™

A good road trip has the following elements: a destination, a map, directions, roadblocks to avoid, pit stops, and sightseeing side trips along the way.

Leading change has similar elements to a road trip:

DESTINATION: the desired business results to be achieved by the change

MAP: the ABC Transition Roadmap™ — the 'mental locations' people will travel through to transition to the future state (it may or may not include the candy cane forest or the Lincoln Tunnel)

DIRECTIONS: AIM Changing Conversations — the specific conversations to facilitate to lead people through the ABC Transition Roadmap™

ROADBLOCKS: the inevitable resistance to the change. See Chapter Three for more on resistance

PIT STOPS AND SIGHTSEEING SIDE TRIPS: see Chapter Seven for more on these

Figure 2.1. The ABC Transition Roadmap™

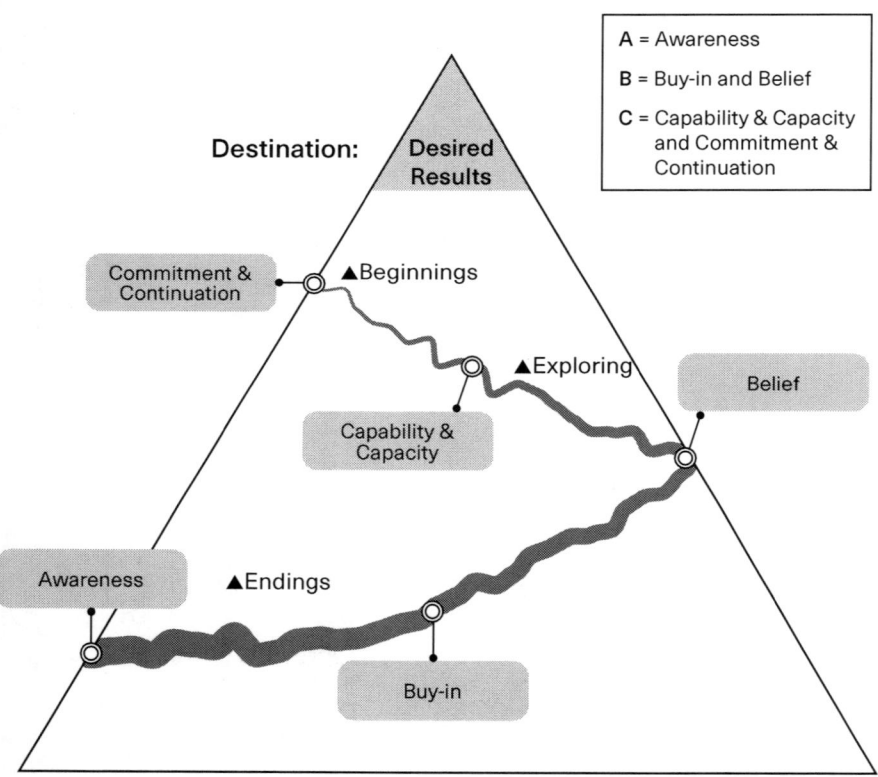

The ABC Transition Roadmap™ has five 'mental locations', or objectives, as shown in Figure 2.1. To lead people through transition successfully, all five objectives must be met. People need to be aware of what is changing, buy into the change, believe that the change is possible, have the capability and capacity to make the change, and ultimately commit to the change and continue making decisions in alignment with the direction of the change. That's it, that's all. How hard can it be? Let's take a closer look.

Awareness

You need to know why change is happening, what is changing, when, and how you are impacted. What's the reason we need to downsize our office space, or implement a new system, or bring in a new leader? Asking "why?" is something we learn early in life but the answer "because I said so" is not likely going to fly with most team members. The right answer is to build awareness through communication and conversation:

- Repeat key messages — *one more time with feeling*
- Alter messages as needed based on feedback
- Provide clarity on why, what, when, how and who the change will impact

Building awareness takes time as people will pay attention when the message is relevant to them. Be patient, communicate regularly, and continue having conversations. See the Communication Planning Conversation in Chapter Eight to develop your communication strategy.

Buy-in

Once you know why something is happening your first thought is often, what does this mean for me, my team, or my business? Once you have a better understanding of the impacts of the change you are more likely to buy in and support the idea of the change. You need to have your thoughts, fears, and ideas acknowledged and validated in order to move on. You need to accept that this change is going to happen. It doesn't mean you are fully committed to it yet, but you are willing to buy into the idea of the change. Leaders need to engage in conversations with their teams to help them understand the impact of the changes to start to create buy-in.

Belief

For any change to happen you have to believe that it is possible. You may need evidence of what is possible. Or perhaps the right inspiration to develop the belief that it is achievable. If you want to run a marathon you have to train, eat right, train some more, and *believe* that you can actually run a marathon. Without belief in the possibility of the future state you will always hold back and not fully commit to the change. If you don't believe that you can actually finish a marathon, you are correct, you will not. Belief is often created with both evidence and inspiration. You may need to see what the new system can do or visit a different manufacturing plant to observe the new equipment in action. You may need to test out the new mountain bike to believe it will handle better than your old bike on single track trails. Seeing is believing, so how can you inspire people with what is possible and show them evidence that it can happen? Belief is also driven by past changes. If the organization has a poor change implementation track record the likelihood of future change success is diminished because people may have lost faith in the leaders' ability to navigate change.

Capability and Capacity

Once people believe they can change, then they need the skills and the opportunity to succeed. You may believe that you can run a marathon but right now you can barely run around the block. To build your capability you must train, and train properly, to improve your chances of success and to realize the change from not being a marathon runner to being a marathon finisher. In organizations this includes training and coaching people to be able to perform new skills and behaviors. People need to feel competent in the new way of doing things.

Having been through many changes myself over the years, I know from personal experience that when something changes my competence level drops, especially when it comes to technology, which I find amusing since I used to implement systems for a living. Many people will go from being competent at their jobs to being incompetent for a period of time during change. They need a safe place to practice, fail, try again, and not be judged along the way. Leaders need to provide the right tools and create the right environment for people to succeed. Adults learn through experimenting and reflecting so allow ample opportunities to learn by doing with feedback and support systems in place.

The second part of this objective is capacity. The opportunity to succeed includes having the right resources to deliver on the future state. This may mean having the right number of people, the right equipment, or the right funding. If your goal is to increase sales by 50% through your sales force and you don't increase the number of salespeople, you are unlikely to realize your goal without burning out your sales team, creating resentment, and risking resignations. Be realistic about the capacity needed to realize your business goals.

Commitment and Continuation

Commitment and continuation are your ultimate 'mental locations' or objectives on the ABC Transition Roadmap™, taking you to the destination of realizing the desired business results. Here you have people committed to the change and continuing to make decisions in alignment with the direction of the change. They buy into it, they believe it, and they are capable of performing in order to achieve the future state. Congratulations!

But don't be fooled, people need a reason to *stay* changed. In other words, to remain in this new state. You want them to commit *and* you want them to continue to work in the new way. You need them to solve problems using the new ideas and the new tools they have learned, and you need them to be able to consistently perform new skills and demonstrate new behaviors.

And let's not confuse commitment with compliance. People who are simply going through the motions of using the new system or following the new procedure will fall back into their old ways the minute you're not looking.

Sustaining commitment and continuing the journey to realize the desired benefits of the change takes both reinforcement *and* a shift in how people are measured and rewarded. You can alter performance measures and rewards to reflect the connection between new behaviors and business success. Alternatively, you can develop succession plans that require demonstrating the new skills and behaviors consistently and effectively in order to be considered for promotions or new roles. The Performance Conversation in Chapter Eight provides more ideas on how to build, reinforce, and sustain the new skills and behaviors needed for commitment and continuation.

People will accelerate at different speeds, each on their own road trip through change.

Remember the marathon effect? As each person travels on their own road trip through change, leaders need to go back to the marathon starting line, find the runners still tying their laces, cheer from the sidelines, and run alongside their team members to help them cross the finish line of change. It will be exciting and rewarding. It will be exhausting and exasperating. You will engage — *one more time with feeling* — until you have your team across the finish line — until the next change! Training for the marathon will give you the stamina to finish the race. Embracing the need for conversations will give you the stamina to lead change every day, because change is here to stay.

One More Time with Feeling

- Individuals need to change in order for the organization to be changed
- Whether change is chosen or imposed, people will experience the Seven Dynamics of Change:
  - Feel awkward and uncomfortable
  - Focus on what they have to give up
  - Feel all alone
  - Can only take so much change
  - Have different levels of readiness
  - Are concerned about not enough resources
  - Revert back to the old way of doing things if not pressured to stay changed
- The ABC Transition Roadmap™ outlines the five objectives to be met to enable people through transitions:
  - Awareness
  - Buy-in
  - Belief
  - Capability and Capacity
  - Commitment and Continuation

The destination is clear, the desired results are well known,

Use the ABCs of transition to lead through the zones,

From endings, to exploring and then onto beginning,

Past the seven dynamics and soon you'll be winning,

But how do you do it? The question remains,

What are the conversations that will lead to change?

Dealing with Resistance

3

AS WE CONTINUE along our road trip through change we will inevitably hit roadblocks — resistance to change. Resistance is a natural response to the endings that occur and to the effort required to adjust to change. Resistance happens whether the change is chosen or imposed. Even chosen changes can evoke resistance because they require adjustment. The severity of resistance depends on our perspective of the possible outcomes and on our willingness and ability to adapt to what's different.

Outcomes often viewed as positive:

1. Increased status – obtaining a new position or new skills

2. Increased career opportunities – improved marketability or advancement opportunities

3. Increased decision-making authority – expanded role or flatter organization

4. Increased stature of the company – becoming a market leader or having cutting-edge offerings

5. Increased productivity – better technology or improved processes

Outcomes often viewed as negative:

1. Loss of competence – no longer being an expert (e.g., when old systems are decommissioned) or taking on an unfamiliar role

2. Loss of control – career path changes or changes in formal or informal authority

3. Loss of relationships – working with new colleagues or reporting to new managers

4. Loss of purpose – new organizational goals

Any of the above can of course be viewed oppositely. I may be thrilled to be working with a new team, however, I still need to go through the growing pains of adjusting to a new structure with new colleagues. I may question why we follow a certain process as I try to understand it better or save files in the wrong spot because I haven't learned where 'the right spot' is yet. While I adjust to what I have gained and lost, my colleagues may view my 'growing pains' as resistance.

What is Lost?

As we've learned, change requires people to go through a psychological process of endings, exploring, and new beginnings. The starting point for dealing with transition is not the outcome but the endings that result when people leave the old world behind. People often look to their jobs for stability: a consistent income, relationships, and routine that is known and comfortable. Change throws this into question and as one of the Seven Dynamics of Change reveals, people tend to focus on what they might lose before thinking about what they might gain. Some of those losses may include:

- Comfort – knowing what to do and how and when to do it
- Turf – authority in certain areas
- Status – job title or access to people and perks
- Alignment to values – the new way may conflict with personal values
- Structure – policies, schedules, deadlines, physical arrangements, performance expectations
- Mastery – expertise in certain areas

- Control – decision authority and knowing priorities
- Purpose – doing meaningful work
- Independence – ability to come and go when desired
- Attachments – a desk, an office, a favorite drink from the coffee machine
- Relationships – coworkers, managers, familiar faces at the food court outlets
- Security – a job, a vacation allotment, a stable income
- Identity – being known for something
- Future – promotions, vacations, salary raises, new opportunities
- Balance – work/life arrangements

Wow! Change sounds terrible when we think about all the things we may lose. You have to help people work through the losses before they can move forward with the change because when losses are not acknowledged or compensated for:

- All positive talk about the new situation is overshadowed by people's focus on losses
- People look for little ways to slow things down, to give themselves time to hold on to pieces of the world they have known
- People may become distrustful and hard to manage

What is Gained?

Gains, like losses, are dependent on what is changing and also on each person's perspective. As much as all the things listed above could be losses, they too could be gains. However, people are generally not as quick to consider what they may gain from a change. And gains may take longer to realize than losses. For example, if you move to a new team the loss of your old relationships is more acute as it takes time to build new relationships. Or the loss of competence in an old system weighs on you as you struggle to decipher the new system and your work takes twice as long.

Remember our story about moving house? We were moving to a bigger, better house in a more desirable neighborhood. By most accounts, this seemed like a positive change. However, it was still disruptive to the current state. As noted before, we had to get used to a new neighborhood, new coffee shop, new neighbors, new places to store things in the house. It altered the status quo and the existing routine, and while it wasn't necessarily a negative thing, it was different, and different takes time to get used to.

Why do People Resist Being Changed?

"*People don't resist change. They resist being changed!*"
Peter Senge

Resistance to being changed is everywhere in our daily lives. Sometimes literally. I remember chasing a soggy-diapered toddler who did not want a diaper change — and many of us have experienced the definitive 'NO' from a four year old who does not want to stop playing at the park to go home for dinner. Whenever change is introduced it threatens what we know, it threatens our current state. And we all know we like things to stay the way they are.

People resist change for three reasons:

1. **They are not aware:** they truly don't know what is changing. They have missed all the emails or meetings about the change or the relevance to them hasn't registered yet.

2. **They are not able:** they do not have the skills to do something differently, or don't believe they are able to make the change.

3. **They are not willing:** they may not agree with the reason for the change or may not feel that the 'why' is compelling enough to change. Not willing can also be a compounding effect of the first two — not aware and not able, then people simply refuse.

In the example of my four year old at the park, she was *able* to leave the park (walk or get a ride in the stroller), she was *aware* of why I wanted to leave the park (to go home for dinner), but she was *not willing*. My reason for change was not compelling enough for her. She was having fun with her friends and, in her mind, leaving the park would change that. How did I eventually get her home? You guessed it — conversations. First with the other mom to agree to leave together, and second with my daughter to explain that her friends were leaving too. Eventually we made it home!

> *It ought to be remembered that there is nothing more difficult to take in hand or more perilous to conduct than to lead the introduction of the new order of things. The innovator has for opposition all those who have done well under the old conditions.*
> Machiavelli

Reasons for Resistance

1. **NOT AWARE:** Lack of awareness is the number one reason why people resist change. It may be that 'I simply don't know that something is different' or I may resist because 'I don't know why something is different'. People get so many emails and memos, the one about the change may have slipped through the cracks.

   I took my girls to swimming lessons one day at a pool we had not been to for close to a year, I hopped into the one lane available to start my own swim lengths for exercise, as I had done the year before whenever they were at lessons. As I was putting on my goggles, I could see a woman, clearly a manager from the front, hustling down the pool deck towards me. She was quite concerned that I was in the pool. Apparently, there was a new rule that, for safety reasons, only children in lessons were allowed in the pool during lesson time. I had no idea this was a new rule. So, where she may have thought I was outright resisting, I in fact just didn't know. I begrudgingly hopped out of the pool and did not return during their lessons. Now I knew the rules and I also knew why there was a rule. Therefore, I changed my behavior.

I previously mentioned the new volunteer sign in process at school. The secretary was frustrated that no one was following the new process. I reminded her that she'd only sent one email about it so far and it happened to be the one that I'd read that week from the school. I suggested that she continue to communicate the new policy in multiple ways. Don't assume people are disregarding the new way, they simply may not know yet! And for some, once people know there is a new process, they will follow it. For others, an explanation of why there is a new policy may be the key to convincing them to change.

> Change? I didn't know.
> Did it get announced?
> I missed the memo!

2. **NOT ABLE**: often with change there are new skills or behaviors expected. When people don't have the skills to perform in the new environment, they may demonstrate resistance in some manner. They may fear they will lose their jobs if they can't learn the new tasks or behave in the new way.

   I worked with Marlene on a project. As the owner of our initiative's website, she was asked to take the lead on migrating content to a new web platform. She did not know how to use the new platform. We had a tight deadline and she told us it couldn't happen. She needed another month to enlist the support of IT. Through one-on-one conversations and prioritizing this project with IT, Marlene was able to learn the new platform and exceeded even her own expectations. Marlene gained the confidence and ability needed to make the changes and helped us achieve the project objectives on time.

3. **NOT WILLING**: in 'not aware' people *didn't know* why change was happening, in 'not willing' they may *not agree* with the 'why'. The

reason to change needs to be more compelling than the reason to remain the same — and a compelling reason to one person may not be as compelling to another person. Or, as noted above, not willing can also be a compounding effect of the first two — not aware and not able, then people simply refuse. Not willing might also be that you have to work with different people now and your past experience working with that team or group may be negative. This is where an open mind is needed to start fresh and let go of past perceptions or experiences.

I coached a leader who developed a new vision for his region. Among the region's team members was Don. Don disagreed with the reason for the new vision. He had worked for the company for 30 years and created a successful business using his own methods and tools. Now this new leader had a new vision — a one team vision. Don's office's client wins and losses would now be part of the greater region's wins and losses. Don was losing control of his corner of the world. He believed that his office's wins and losses should remain just that, his. The region leader spent time with Don, he learned the history of the office and region — a change like this had been done before that resulted in Don losing his bonus and two of his staff because another office missed its targets, impacting the whole region. He was definitely once bitten and twice shy. Through many conversations and demonstration of the how the new way was bringing in new and profitable work for everyone, Don eventually bought into the new vision and slowly worked his way to commitment.

> A compelling why and a crystal clear reason, keeps resistance at bay, at least for this season.

Resistance is normal and inevitable.

Resistance isn't necessarily a sign that people are disloyal or looking to impact you negatively. It may simply mean there is more explanation or conversation needed as people adjust to a new reality. And yes, you *will* have the conversations — *one more time with feeling*. Cause for concern is when you seemingly have no resistance. Since resistance is inevitable, it's likely gone underground and will rear its head when you least want it. Resistance will not go away if ignored, it will only get worse if people don't have an outlet to express their feelings.

What Does Resistance Look Like?

Future Shock (coined by Alvin Toffler in 1970) is the point in time when people can no longer assimilate or absorb change without displaying dysfunctional behavior. Knowing that change is constant in today's organizations, the risk of Future Shock is high due to the compounding effect of multiple change efforts. You may have one major change that is impacting the entire organization, for example, rolling out a new enterprise software, but each function is also likely going through its own changes — new leaders, new teammates, new processes, increased workloads, reduced workforce, and more. How do you know when you've hit that boiling point? When the following dysfunctional behaviors occur:

- Passive aggression
- Absenteeism
- Sabotage of relationships or property
- Abusive behavior to self or others

Hopefully you can head off the boiling point behaviors by noticing — and addressing — the emergence of the following resistance behaviors first:

- Complacency, such as saying nothing at all in meetings
- Closed-door meetings on the rise
- Less conversation in the hallways or over online social channels
- Push back in meetings and/or accusatory questions
- Disagreements
- Telling customers about organizational dysfunction
- Doing the minimum and not putting in any extra effort

Some of these actions are contradictory, but based on the knowledge of your team, you'll notice what is different — are they talking more or less, producing better results or not. If the changes in behavior persist, it's time to address it.

The Impact of Unaddressed Resistance

Hoping resistance will go away will not make it so. Nor will simply employing more cheerleaders to tout the greatness of your change. You must address the areas of resistance and if you don't, this change and future changes will be in jeopardy.

Current changes may not be realized because:

1. People simply don't change their behavior.

2. They find ways to get around the change (e.g., getting others to update the new accounting system versus learning to do it themselves).

3. They accept only part of the change which causes more work for others (e.g., saving files in the right place but not using the right templates).

4. Business is disrupted to a greater degree than anticipated (e.g., the technology doesn't do what it was supposed to; therefore, people spend extra time to do the same work).

5. Resources (time, money, people) are wasted — people get frustrated or money runs out before finishing the change properly.

6. Morale declines in the face of too much change — people are overwhelmed.

7. New opportunities are missed as people spend too much time trying to make the change.

Future change efforts are jeopardized because:

1. They require more money that isn't available.

2. People lose confidence in leaders.

3. Old ways of doing things become more entrenched.

4. Resistance increases as people have negative memories of the last time a change was introduced.

Although it can be tempting to avoid people who are resisting, going through emotional times, or aren't seeming to respond rationally, it's important not to ignore or avoid them. The COVID-19 crisis put this front and center in our household. With two children needing to continue their schoolwork remotely it was often a struggle to keep them motivated, let alone happy about homeschooling. Our teaching and coaching efforts were often met with grumpy behavior. It would have been easier to let them skip their schoolwork and sulk in their rooms by themselves, but we knew that that was not the answer. Although rewarding melt-down behavior was not what we wanted to do, we knew that some time spent outside or biking with friends (at a distance) would restore some sense of normalcy and contentment. So, we organized socially distant activities and stayed connected with our children through conversations. It was a bumpy road at times, but necessary in the face of change.

I have a colleague who loves to say "move quickly and don't make eye contact" — perhaps a good motto for catching your commuter train on time, but not a great change strategy. You have to slow down, make eye contact, connect with people so they feel heard, be curious. Uncover the real reasons for their resistance and find solutions that will work not only for them, but for the organization too.

As noted above, negative memories of past changes can lead to increased resistance to future changes. Taking the time to address resistance will enable the success of your current change and facilitate future changes as well.

Not Everyone Will Resist!

Not all resistance will result in the feeling of pushing water uphill. We know that people will go through a predictable pattern of reactions — the Seven Dynamics of Change — as they move from endings, to exploring, to the new beginning, but for some people those phases will happen quickly and they will be ready to move on.

Conversations and Strategies to Address Resistance

To overcome resistance to change people need to have the will, the skill, and the opportunity to do something different.

	WILLING TO CHANGE	NOT WILLING TO CHANGE
ABLE	Leader — willingly accepts change, may be the one initiating the change ideas	Hesitant resistor — needs motivation and opportunity for success to move forward
NOT ABLE	Embracer — willing to change and needs information and training to move forward	Persistent resistor — if AIM Changing Conversations don't work, may need to be removed

The following conversations will help you uncover resistance and address it (see Part Three for detailed outlines of these conversations):

1. THE STAKEHOLDER CONVERSATION – when planning the change, anticipate why people might resist and develop mitigation strategies.

2. THE DEBRIEF CONVERSATION, THE IMPACT CONVERSATION, THE CHANGE TRACK RECORD CONVERSATION – provide opportunities for people to articulate their concerns and frustrations.

3. THE PERSONAL CHANGE JOURNEY CONVERSATION – help people build their own self-awareness about their reactions to change.

4. **THE STOP, START, CONTINUE CONVERSATION** – help people prioritize their work.

5. **THE COACHING CONVERSATION** – help people understand expectations and provide one-on-one support.

6. **THE CELEBRATION AND THANK YOU CONVERSATION** – celebrate wins to build momentum.

7. **THE ARE YOU ON BOARD? CONVERSATION** – set expectations and provide specific feedback about resistant behaviors.

Beyond specific actions resulting from your conversations, your strategies to address resistance may include:

- Giving people a specific role in the change — either as part of the larger initiative or something specific to their team (e.g., create new processes or standards aligned to the change).

- Leveraging certain resistors as part of a champion network to use their energy for good instead of evil!

- Where possible and appropriate, removing people from the team or organization.

Ready to plan your conversations? Learn how to prepare and facilitate the right conversations in Part Two.

Take the time to get to know why people resist. Time spent one-on-one can result in a shift.

Addressing resistance is one of the key areas for conversations, and a big opportunity for one-on-one conversations. I have worked with countless people who demonstrate resistance in group meetings. They give the reasons why something can't be done, why it won't work, and why we don't have enough resources to make it happen anyway. That's when you know it's time to end the meeting and follow up with this person directly. My experience has taught me that this behavior is about not wanting to set expectations they can't meet.

Take Luke for example. Luke was an IT guy at one of my clients. He was the one who developed the system that had been used in his organization for years. The time had come to replace the system — clearly a threat to his expertise. It turned out that he was also quite adept at using the new system but in meetings he'd say that things couldn't be done how we wanted. I stopped by Luke's office one day to check these assumptions and to uncover his real resistance. A one-on-one conversation gave me the chance to get to know Luke, I learned about his background with the organization and built rapport with him. This was a variation of the Are You on Board? Conversation (see Chapter Nine) and it helped me better understand his resistance to the change.

As my conversation with Luke continued I came to realize that he could, in fact, do what we were asking, he had thought of it long before we had, but he was unsure if he could produce the desired results or if he could do it in time. Mystery solved, I understood his resistance, I figured out a way to engage him in the larger group conversations with minimal outward resistance, and he delivered what we needed!

One More Time with Feeling

- People focus first on what they perceive they will lose during change and losses are perceived differently by each person.
- Resistance is inevitable during change.
- People resist because they are: (1) not aware of the change, (2) not able, or believe they are not able, to perform due to the change, or (3) not willing to change.
- Unaddressed resistance will impact current change efforts and future change efforts.
- Ignoring resistance will not make it go away.
- Uncover and manage resistance through conversations — in groups and one-on-one.

Resistance, alas it must be addressed,

So, uncover the causes of why folks are stressed,

Not aware, not able, not willing, oh my,

The perception of loss, or not agreeing with why,

Through conversations the reasons will all become clear,

Then you can plan a path forward with less worry and fear.

PART TWO

AIM Changing Conversations: The Why, How, What, and Who

Why Conversations are Needed

4

AS WE SAW with the ABC Transition Roadmap™ in Chapter Two and addressing resistance in Chapter Three, transforming an organization requires people to commit to the change. Commitment is gained when people feel heard. People feel heard when they are engaged in productive conversations. Conversations get the thoughts out of our heads. Thoughts lead to emotions. Emotions lead to actions. Actions lead to results.

Conversations are the gateway through which people move from awareness, to buy-in, to belief, and ultimately to committing to and continuing a change. To change, people need to see things from different perspectives and conversations help them do this. People need a safe place when transitioning from the current state to the future state, they need to be able to express their feelings, relate to others, share similar experiences, and process new information. So, it's time to start *Talking Change*, *with* people, not *at* people.

> If you have to guess, you can't address. If you don't know what people are thinking (positive or negative) you can't act on it. Start the conversation.

Conversations create change.

A conversation is described in the Merriam-Webster dictionary as an oral exchange of sentiments, observations, opinions, or ideas. If we dissect this, we see that a conversation is oral, therefore, good conversation does not happen over email or text or via a memo. A conversation involves an exchange, thus it's two-way, not just a one-way presentation with no interaction. I'm a fan of face-to-face conversations. However, when that is not possible, virtual meetings work too — or simply pick up the phone. Remember when people used to do that?

Conversations can be short, but impactful. "Will you marry me?", "Yes". Think of some impactful conversations you've had in your life. Can you think of one situation where there was no conversation before you decided to take action? Before you say yes, don't forget that conversations with yourself count as conversations. Standing at the top of a never-before-skied-by-me run that looks too steep, too bumpy, too icy, and too daunting requires a conversation with myself — *one more time with feeling* — before I point my skies downhill and move. Conversations can solve problems, enlighten thinking, move us to action, and yes, create change.

AIM Changing Conversations

Everyday we have multiple conversations on a wide variety of topics from work, to family, to events, to the weather. The conversations outlined in this book are to help those charged with leading their teams and employees through change. I call these AIM Changing Conversations. A play on game-changing and the company name I created years ago. Action Impact Movement. Commit to action. Make an impact. Create the movement. Still words I live by to help create change.

AIM Changing Conversations are planned and facilitated conversations with groups or one-on-one to drive change. But don't underestimate the opportunity to influence change during a one-off hallway or ski lift conversation. How many times have you received a recommendation or an idea from someone in a random conversation that has led you to change dry cleaners, try a new restaurant, or find out more?

What was the last conversation you had that compelled you to change your perspective? Or commit to a change? Or believe that there really was a better way?

To drive change we need to **engage in AIM Changing Conversations — to be curious and create common understanding** — through each stage of the transition process to build awareness and ultimately gain commitment to change. Preparing for and practicing these conversations will improve your everyday impromptu conversations as well.

Recently I worked with a team on capital projects. During our usual Status and Progress Conversation (see Chapter Eight) the meeting was sidetracked by a current issue. We refocused our discussion on that issue. What I discovered is that the team struggled to discuss their different perspectives effectively on the issue and couldn't come to a conclusion on what to do next.

We took a step back, identified the real issues, the risks, and the urgency of the needed fix. During the discussion I asked them questions about the specifics of the problem, their immediate response was that I didn't need to know the specifics. I pointed out that my curiosity was not for my benefit, it was so that everyone in the room had a common understanding of the situation.

This team was known for performing procedures slightly differently on different shifts. By answering my questions they were seeing different points of view and gaining a complete picture of the issue. Once we agreed on the magnitude of the problem and the potential risks, we were able to brainstorm viable solutions to the problem. The understanding in the room increased and stress levels decreased, all

> Engage in AIM Changing Conversations to create common ground; to be curious, to learn and to question, then understand, and pick a direction.

because of an AIM Changing Conversation. This conversation was a step forward in the team being able to create change and solve more problems together in the future.

The Benefits of Conversations

THOUGHTS BECOME WORDS: I've been a coach for many years. I've coached people to earn promotions, develop better business plans, manage teams more effectively, lead change, and, at times, to get out of their own way. Coaching clearly involves conversation. One thing I've realized with coaching is that when you say something out loud it sounds much different than it does in your head. When we verbalize our thoughts we see them for what they really are — good ideas, ridiculous ideas, ideas that need tweaking, or really bad ideas. In our heads we justify, we protect, we spin and spiral, and we make it hard for others to understand our perspectives.

> Get it out of your head and have it said.

FEELINGS ARE UNCOVERED: not every leader signed up to deal with people's feelings and emotions. But as it turns out, humans aren't robots. Successful change requires successful transition — an internal psychological journey involving feelings. Finding out how people feel about the change, the actions being taken, and the desired end state, will help you chart your path to success. Conversations will uncover what is really going on. Are people angry, sad, frustrated, excited, or concerned, and why are they feeling those emotions? Feelings are often triggered by people's values. When someone's values are being trampled on they get frustrated, sad, or angry. Gently dig into those feelings to find out what's really going on because what they say initially is not always the full picture.

> When feelings are known, understanding is grown.

ASSUMPTIONS ARE ERODED: shockingly, our assumptions are not always correct. We make assumptions based on our frame of reference. Our frame of reference is created by our experiences, our knowledge, our values, and beliefs. We assume something about someone based on what we see on the outside — their behavior (e.g., absenteeism), their actions (e.g., closed doors), or overheard comments in the lunch room. Being in conversation — listening, learning, and asking questions — creates the opportunity to challenge our assumptions, get to know people better, and find out what is real versus what we assumed.

> If you assume without asking, your interpretation is lacking.

PERCEPTIONS ARE CHANGED: "once in a while you get shown the light, in the strangest of places if you look at it right." Not only a Grateful Dead lyric, it's also a great change strategy. Everyone has a different perspective on what is changing, this perspective is part of what impacts their readiness for and reactions to change. Conversation is the vehicle to understanding others' perspectives and often, overcoming resistance. Understanding different perspectives will enable you to uncover resistance, find leaders that you didn't expect, and discover ideas in unusual places. Conversations also shine the spotlight on your own perspective, providing the opportunity to examine it and possibly change not only your perspective but that of others as well. To transition through change there is a pretty good chance that you will need to change people's perspectives. I do an exercise I call 'through others' eyes' when

> Once in while you get shown the light, in the strangest of places if you look at it right.
> The Grateful Dead

working with teams on strategic planning. Once they land on the big initiatives they want to implement in the coming year, they take on the roles of different functions. What will HR or IT or Finance think of these initiatives? How will the initiatives impact the different groups? What will employees think? They change their perspectives and they see something different, often causing the team to tweak their thinking. Change your perspective and change what you see.

COMMON UNDERSTANDING PREVAILS: the purpose of being curious in conversations is to come to a common understanding. This doesn't mean agreement in all cases, it means interpretations move closer into alignment. Conversation enables us to ask questions until we gain a common understanding. And one conversation may not be enough for this. Once I spent an hour on the phone with a colleague to develop a tracking chart. I thought our understanding of the chart was aligned at the end of the call. When he sent the chart, I knew I was wrong. It did not reflect my interpretation of the conversation. So — *one more time with feeling* — we delved into the details, asked each other questions, and eventually came to a common understanding.

> Understanding is needed, but not always in sync. We need to converse to know what each other thinks.

COMMUNITY IS CREATED: conversations connect people during change. It's an opportunity to realize that you are not going through the change alone. The more everyone truly feels like they are going through the change together, the better the chance of making it successful. I worked on the merger of two travel companies — SunHere and SandThere. They both moved into SunHere's building and adopted one reservation system — an upgrade of SunHere's current system. The Operations teams of the two companies were located on different floors. While the SunHere team easily transitioned to the new system, the SandThere team struggled. In a simple, yet powerful move, we created the opportunity for conversations by moving both Operations teams to the same floor; employees from each company were now sitting together and having conversations to get to know each other and learn from each other. The co-location created the opportunity for conversation and the conversations created a community. They realized they were in this merger together. Creating the opportunity for conversation and

> Shuffle the space to spend time face-to-face.

collaboration is key during change. Most people will not make the first move so as a leader you need to make it happen.

DECISIONS ARE REACHED: conversations are key to getting people to decide if they are 'in or out' when it comes to change. People need to take in information, have the opportunity to ask questions and come to their own conclusions about the change — do they buy in, do they believe it's possible, will they commit to what's needed for success? Being in conversation enables people to gather information to make choices and to see what choices they have.

> I ask, I ponder, I may have doubts. I listen then decide if I'm in or out.

CONFIDENCE IS INCREASED: the more conversations you facilitate, the more confident you will become at facilitating conversations. The extroverts reading this are on board, the introverts, maybe not so much, but with some structure and willingness to engage, your confidence will grow! And your confidence as the leader is not the only benefit. The more opportunities people have to discuss, ask questions, and hear about what is changing, the more their confidence will grow in how you are leading the change. Note that I said in how you are leading the change and not necessarily confidence in what is actually changing. I've worked with leaders who've had changes imposed on them that have totally gone off the rails — system delays, organizational issues, etc. — yet the leaders engaged in conversations with their teams to alleviate fears, understand perspectives, and identify a good path forward, despite the issues with the change. These conversations helped the employees feel confident that their leaders had their best interest at heart.

> Practice makes perfect, though perfection's not needed. Gaining confidence is key, don't be defeated.

NEW BEHAVIORS ARE DEMONSTRATED: consistently demonstrating new behavior is important on the path to change and doing so in your conversations is a great place to start. If the leader isn't acting in the new way, then why should their employees? People need a reason to stay changed. For anyone who is a parent, you know that children mimic their parents, just like employees mimic the behavior of their leaders. I've learned about some of my bad habits by seeing them acted out by the mirrors that are my children! Staying changed is hard for everyone, and as we said before, change is initially awkward and uncomfortable, so acting in the new way will be uncomfortable to start. You might be using new sales language in a meeting when others give you quizzical looks. The temptation is to revert back to the old way, but alas, you must push ahead. Role model the new way, push through the awkwardness, and gather others into your tent as you go. The fact that you're engaging in conversations may be new behavior in your organization. Be the pied piper with your head held high. Use the new technology, bring people into conversation, follow the new volunteer process of signing in and wearing a bright blue badge! Be consistent in using the new behaviors and others will join you, and feel less awkward when they have a leader to follow.

> Show me first, then I'll follow. But be consistent or I'll see your acts as hollow.

The Sticky Side of Conversations

It sounds magical, that one or two conversations can get everyone aligned and rowing in the same direction. But our experience tells us that this likely won't happen. We've all been in a conversation that's gone sideways. A question you ask sparks an inflammatory response, then others jump on the negative train of thought and all of a sudden anarchy erupts in the room. Or people start crying and the leader clams up, not knowing how to handle intense emotions. Or, the audience goes completely silent, fearing there will be ramifications if they voice their true thoughts and feelings. I've seen leaders shy away from asking any questions, thus stunting all conversation in the room. The leader feels like they have 'dodged a bullet' by keeping the negativity and emotion out of the room; however, that negativity will surface — in the hallways, behind closed doors, in text messages — and start to fester. This is when the rumor mill gets started — people make assumptions because they didn't get their questions answered in the meeting. They test their assumptions with others, and suddenly, rumors are flying around like Hogwarts students on broomsticks. Enabling the conversation to happen with the right people in the room will improve your chances of building common understanding and minimizing how many rumors you need to manage after the fact.

Before engaging in a potentially sticky conversation, consider connecting with your inner circle of peers, mentors, or coaches. These people can give you a good idea of possible reactions, what questions may come up, and their thoughts on possible answers to those questions. Engaging in these pre-conversations can minimize your anxiety about leading sticky conversations. You can also draw on these people for support if they are part of the group conversations. Not all conversations are going to be easy, but you have to jump in, be courageous and demonstrate empathy and kindness during your conversations.

One More Time with Feeling

AIM Changing Conversations are needed to create common understanding and to help people through transition.

Conversations create change. By engaging in conversations you will:

- Put words to thoughts
- Uncover feelings
- Erode assumptions
- Change perceptions
- Create common understanding
- Build community

- Reach decisions
- Increase confidence
- Demonstrate new behavior

Jack is resilient, Jill is quick, conversations have helped their team make changes that stick,

Conversation creates the chance to ask and exchange, the thoughts and the feelings you have about change,

To now understand, the reasons for why, the change must occur, and you need not only comply,

But buy in and believe, commit and continue, to adapt and be nimble and embrace what is new.

How to Lead Conversations

5

Conversation Cornerstones

The goal of AIM Changing Conversations is to be curious and create common understanding as people travel along the ABC Transition Roadmap™. Personal transition, which we've learned is necessary for successful change, doesn't happen because of a project plan. It happens when people feel heard and seen. Everyone has a decision to make during change — to do or not do. Facilitating conversations to help people make decisions in alignment with the direction you want to go will improve your chances of successful change. To engage others effectively in conversation, we need to follow a few guidelines, I refer to these as the Conversation Cornerstones. These are not new concepts; you've likely learned them before, but we need to remind ourselves to abide by these cornerstones during our conversations.

BE PRESENT: focus on what is happening in the conversation, and only on what is happening in the conversation, not on your next meeting or what you are going to have for lunch. People know when you're not paying attention. Being present takes practice. If you have ever pursued mindfulness or meditation you know that the experience of being present takes work and focus. When your mind wanders you miss important nuances that provide insight into people's perspectives and how they are *really* feeling. Being aware of what is going on during the conversation — what's being said, how it's being said, the mood, and physical cues, will also allow you to manage the environment and adjust as needed. People may feel vulnerable during the conversation, so you need to be aware of what is happening and continually adapt to create a safe space for people to voice their views or ask questions.

ASK GREAT QUESTIONS AND LISTEN ACTIVELY: ask better questions, get better answers. Open-ended questions (those that can't simply be answered with yes or no) will provide richer conversation, though there might be times when a yes or no answer is required, such as seeking agreement or confirmation. What constitutes a great question? Something that will provoke thought, generate ideas, unearth feelings, change perspectives, promote learning, or result in action. I'll provide examples in future chapters. Two of my favorite conversation prompts are: help me understand and tell me more (or tell me what you need to make this change). They aren't questions but they do provoke conversation.

The other trick to asking great questions is listening! Listen for understanding, for emotions and feelings, and for what I call the 'juicy words'. Juicy words are the words that open up the opportunity for further conversation. For example, if someone says, "I can't do that", you can explore the juicy word 'can't' — what makes them believe they can't do it. Listen to the answers, listen for their reasoning and their point of view. Listening will give you clues to formulate your next great question and the next great question may be the one that finally uncovers people's true thoughts and feelings or sparks new ideas. Don't just listen for a pause in the conversation so you can jump back in with your own opinions.

LEARN: all participants will hopefully learn something from each conversation, whether that is knowledge about the change, understanding of different perspectives, or new information about each other. Eventually each person needs to decide if they will commit to the change or not.

Learning will create common understanding and will help people come to their own conclusions and make their own decisions.

TAKE ACTION: decisions, next steps, action items, further conversation, or simply reflecting on what was discussed. Some sort of action must be prompted from the conversation and agreed to by participants. We've all attended meetings with no apparent resolution or direction at the end. The purpose of some of your conversations will simply be to listen and let people feel heard. However, it's still important to discuss next steps. Summarize the discussion, thank participants for their time and input, and commit to what's next.

Conversation Planner

The thought of facilitating conversations sparks excitement in some people and dread in others. As a leader during change, the fact is you will need to engage in conversations. Planning for these conversations will help you stay on track, minimize tangents, ensure that the conversation is productive, and feel more comfortable and confident — even for those who would rather crawl under their desk and hide than facilitate a conversation.

Employing the Conversation Cornerstones will help you *during* a conversation. Using the Conversation Planner will help you prepare *before* you start a conversation.

See the sample completed Conversation Planner below and the blank template in Appendix A. You can also download the Conversation Planner at www.actionimpactmovement.com/resources

When planning your conversation, consider:

PURPOSE: what are the outcomes you are hoping to achieve? What do want people to know, do, or feel by the end of the meeting? What information, insight, or input do you want from the audience?

AUDIENCE: who will be involved in the conversation? What are the unique characteristics of this group? What do you know about this audience that will impact your conversation (i.e., what do they know already about your topic, do you expect resistance to your topic, etc.)?

TIMING: when does the conversation need to happen? Right after an announcement or action (e.g., training)? Before an announcement (e.g., prepare leaders before announcing something to the entire organization)?

SIZE: how many people will be part of this conversation? The size of the group will impact how you facilitate the conversation.

LOCATION: are you meeting on the phone, in person, via an online meeting platform? Where are people located? Are they all together or dispersed?

LOGISTICS: how will you engage people in conversation? One-on-one, small groups, large group, using polls or voting, using a specific facilitation method, etc? How will you create the environment for optimal contribution to the conversation (i.e., how will you make people feel safe to share their views)?

QUESTIONS: based on the meeting goals, how will you set context for the conversation? What questions do you want to ask the group? In what order will you ask your questions? Select questions from the AIM Changing Conversations in Part Three.

REACTIONS: anticipate possible responses to your questions. Generate a list of questions people may ask during the conversation and consider your answers ahead of time.

Conversation Planner Example

CONVERSATION	THE IMPACT CONVERSATION
Purpose	Identify the possible impact of the changes on our team
Audience	Operations team
Timing	Week of July 15 (change was announced on July 5)
Size	15 people, including leader
Location	All attendees will be remote, attending via online meeting
Logistics	Facilitated by external facilitator. Large group using anonymous polling questions and/or whiteboard. Then small breakout groups for discussions with selected team members as group hosts. Groups will be assigned, with a mix of junior and senior employees in each one. Team leader will not be part of one of the small groups, will be part of large group discussions/polls.
Questions	Large group — for anonymous responses through whiteboard feature: • What changes do you think will have the biggest impact on our team, in terms of changes to our processes, structure, governance, technology, or outputs? Breakout groups questions: • What do you feel you will lose due to this change? • What is ending with this change? • What do you believe you/our team will gain from this change? Back in the large group — answers in the chat (not anonymous) • What will you/our team need to do differently to execute on the changes?
Reactions	Questions people may have and answers: • When is the change happening? Answer: starting in May • Will anyone lose their job? Answer: No one is slated to lose their job due to this change. Performance will continue to be reviewed as normal and any staffing decisions will be considered based on performance, as is the current practice.

Conversation Agenda

Based on your answers to the above, draft an agenda (with timing and at least some of the key questions). Send the agenda to participants ahead of time. People like to know why they are being invited to a meeting and what will be discussed. It also gives them time to consider their answers prior to the meeting, enabling them to better participate during the meeting. A sample agenda template is located in Appendix B. You can also download a template at www.actionimpactmovement.com/resources

Conversation Considerations

Here are some highlights from my Facilitation Skills Foundations course to keep in mind when facilitating AIM Changing Conversations.

CONNECT WHERE PEOPLE FEEL CONFIDENT: bringing people from the manufacturing plant floor into the main boardroom will likely intimidate them and prevent them from providing the input and suggestions you may be seeking. Go to them. Visit the plant floor, the field office, the retail branch. Go to the place where they are comfortable and confident and where you can see what really happens 'away from head office'. On their own turf they will be more willing and able to show you and tell you their ideas of what can be made better, what's not working, and how to fix it. I have run brainstorming sessions on plant floors, with flip charts and standing meetings. The plant supervisors pointed out the problems, discussed their solution ideas, and the rest of the employees on the plant floor saw that their supervisors were being listened to by senior leaders. We came up with more and better ideas than we would have sitting in the boardroom.

> Learn more by walking the floor.

EXPLAIN HOW INFORMATION WILL BE USED: not everyone will feel comfortable sharing their views or perspectives. Explain how the information they share will be used and what the personal implications will be (if any) for providing specific, and perhaps negative, feedback (e.g., only themes will be shared versus individual views). Then follow through on what you promise. Consider how you will ensure that all voices are heard. You may need to do some one-on-one conversations prior to the large group conversations or have ways for people to share their views anonymously, yet still feed into the overall conversation.

BUILD TRUST: conversations are an opportunity to build trust among teams and with leaders. As people get to know each other better they are more likely to trust each other and start to rely on one another for support through the change. And, as leaders share their ideas, their concerns, and their vulnerabilities, trust in the leaders will grow.

KEEP AN OPEN MIND: even though you have planned your questions and process, you don't know what people might say in the discussion. You are there to learn from others and create common understanding. Keep your judgements to yourself, imposing judgements will stunt the conversation. Keep an open mind and encourage others to do so as well. You want to hear different points of view so you can address questions, uncover resistance, and find new ideas. If all you get is an echo chamber of agreement you're likely missing some important information.

SPEAK THEIR LANGUAGE: start with, "Hi, I'm from head office and I'm here to help," if you want to cue the eye rolls from your audience. Learn the business of the business — build your understanding of the audience, know what's important to them, and what challenges they face everyday. Using terms, phrases, or language that the audience doesn't understand will not promote conversation. Demonstrating your understanding of their world will make them more likely to share their thoughts and ideas. This is also about removing barriers. In workplaces where not everyone is fluent in the primary language used to conduct business, be mindful of helping people contribute their views — speak slowly, have translators, use pictures, or find other ways to ensure people can understand and be understood.

EMPATHIZE: as we've learned, change can cause great uncertainty and emotions. Demonstrate empathy for what your audience is going through, be prepared for emotional reactions, be supportive, but remember, they are not your emotions to own. You cannot control other people's reactions or emotions. You can provide the opportunity for people to discuss their reactions and then make their own choices.

CONTINUE THE CONVERSATION: once the conversation stops, so does the learning. Guide the discussion and don't lead with no. What can you say "yes and" to that will bring more people into the conversation? Create an environment conducive to conversation; this may mean breaking into smaller groups (people are more likely to talk to one or two other people versus to a large group) or switching up your questions.

MONITOR YOUR OWN BEHAVIOR: how you facilitate the conversation will impact the overall mood. Your goal is to encourage others to speak. Monitor how much you are saying, what you are saying, and how you are saying it. It's not just what you say, it's how you say it. I use this line with my daughters when they ask seemingly innocuous questions with an edge. Like when "why is the bathroom light on?" (read with a snarky tone) becomes an accusation versus a simple question.

CONSIDER DIFFERENT PERSONALITY TYPES: different people engage in conversations in different ways. Some like to prepare ahead of time, some like to react in the moment; some like facts and logic, others like to see the impact on people; some like the details, others like the big picture. Know that you will have a combination of people in the conversation and keep this in mind when preparing your questions and any information you may share. For more information on personality types, see Chapter Seven.

SOLVE THE RIGHT PROBLEM: as a consultant I was always taught to come with solutions, not just problems. However, you first need to know which problems you have before you can solve them. Solving the first problem you find may not solve the bigger issue at hand. For example, you may replace the toner in the printer because it's empty, but the bigger problem is too much unnecessary printing. Continue the conversations to ensure you have identified the right problem to solve first.

HAVE FUN: yes, really. Change is a difficult time for many people, with many emotions. Finding a way to have a little fun and create some smiles during some of your conversations will lighten the mood and help people take a different perspective. Change is hard, and if we constantly focus on the negative emotions it will be even harder. There are ways to find some fun even in the midst of change, and it's necessary to find something to smile about to build the stamina to keep going. Find the fun, in the right way. This might be delicious treats at a meeting, it might be ice breakers that uncover people's hidden talents, it might be reminiscing about good times, or the occasional rhyme! I worked with a leader once during a very stressful business transaction and there were many things out of our control. We used to make 'napkin bets', predictions of when or what things would happen written on napkins, nothing malicious, just something to lighten the stress levels. When the events we bet on came to pass we'd pull out the napkins and see who guessed right, and smile every time. Another team I worked with set up a closed social media hub where they would share fun facts and photos with each other. Don't be afraid to have some fun *with* others — but never at their expense.

Conversations happen all the time. The question is, are you leading the type of conversations that will create a positive change?

My experience in many workplaces is that people often struggle to have useful conversations with each other. Your organization will become more nimble when you increase the conversation capability of your people. This skill will enable people to solve problems more effectively, and if they can solve problems together, then they can create radical organizational change too!

From one-on-one informal conversations, to large group facilitations, each conversation is an opportunity to lead by example and propel change forward. Prepare, practice, participate, repeat. Engage in AIM Changing Conversations with curiosity and to create common understanding. Be present, ask great questions and listen, learn, and take action.

One More Time with Feeling

The Conversation Cornerstones and Conversation Considerations will enable you to lead conversations that create change.

Be present

Ask great questions & listen actively

Connect where people feel confident

Have fun

Build trust

Explain how information will be used

Keep an open mind

AIM CHANGING CONVERSATIONS

Be curious and create common understanding

Solve the right problem

Speak their language

Consider different personality types

Empathize

Monitor your own behavior

Continue the conversation

Learn

Take action

64

Now you know all the tips to prepare, plan, and lead,

The conversations to create the dialogue that you need,

To move people, not cheese — remember that fable?

Flip the page for the list of what and who to enable.

What Conversations to Have and with Whom

6

WE'RE READY TO engage in AIM Changing Conversations! As a leader accountable for the success of the change within your organization, you will have loads of conversations, with different people or the same people — *one more time with feeling.*

Remember the marathon effect — as a leader you generally get information earlier than the majority of employees, or may have been part of the change planning process, so keep this in mind when you speak with others who are receiving the information for the first time. You may feel like you are having the same conversation repeatedly, and you are, but each time it will help the same person, or new people, move along their personal change journey to embracing the new beginning.

I taught fitness classes for years, back when choreographed step and 'hi lo' classes were popular. Every week I taught generally the same moves. I was somewhat bored of the routine but every week there were new participants in the class or returning participants who managed to string together more moves, more fluidly, each time they came. I repeated the same moves, with minor additions each week, and by the end of the session the class was synchronized and all following my lead! AIM Changing Conversations are like that fitness class experience. You will continue to have the same or similar conversations and eventually your team will be synchronized in executing the change and realizing the desired results!

What Conversations are Needed?

The following 20 AIM Changing Conversations provide a solid foundation to lead change successfully. In Part Three, I include detailed outlines and questions for each of the conversations. There are ideas for more conversation starters and questions in Appendix C.

SELF-REFLECTION CONVERSATIONS – to realize your personal reactions and responses to change and decide how you will approach future changes:

1. The Personality Preferences Conversation

2. The Personal Change Journey Conversation

3. The Prepare Yourself to Lead Change Conversation

PLANNING AND MANAGING CONVERSATIONS – to decide, organize, plan and manage change initiatives:

1. The Why Conversation

2. The What, When, and How Conversation

3. The Situation Conversation

4. The Stakeholder Conversation

5. The Coordinate Your Asks Conversation

6. The Communication Planning Conversation

7. The Performance Conversation

8. The Status and Progress Conversation

9. The Results Conversation

ENGAGEMENT CONVERSATIONS – to win people's hearts and minds to transform your organization:

1. The Debrief Conversation

2. The Impact Conversation

3. The Change Track Record Conversation

4. The Stop, Start, Continue Conversation

5. The Coaching Conversation

6. The Are You on Board? Conversation

7. The Lessons Learned Conversation

8. The Celebration and Thank You Conversation

Who Needs to Be in Conversation?

Whoever needs to do something more, better, or different needs to be in conversation. To move the organization, the individuals need to move first. Groups will be impacted differently by change and each individual will have a different reaction to change. Depending on your role in the change, you will engage in many of the above conversations. The key roles include:

1. **YOURSELF:** the first conversation is with yourself. Whether you are the initiator or the receiver of the change, you need to understand your own enablers — what will compel you to make the change, and your obstacles — what might hold you back from embracing the change. You may play more than one of the following roles in the change, so it's important to know your personal reactions first.

2. **SPONSORS:** those initiating the change and ultimately responsible for the impact of the change on the organization, but not usually the ones managing the day-to-day change efforts. Sponsors need to be willing to take the risk of putting their ideas out there, with a high likelihood of being opposed on the first pass. They need to craft

a compelling why — the reason they are driving this change. The sponsors will be the first people to run the marathon of transition, so they definitely need to have conversations — *one more time with feeling* — as they bring others on board to their ideas. Sponsors need to gain input and commitment from all their senior management team in order to lead change successfully. They need to involve the right people who have knowledge, resources, and influence to lead the change over the long haul. Dissension in the senior ranks will trickle down throughout the organization. The sponsors need to be aligned on their vision for change, visibility support the change, and inspire confidence that the change is the right thing to do. The team of sponsors who decided on the change must commit to a common goal and relentlessly move forward. Relentlessly does not mean steam-rolling over people to comply with the changes, we know this doesn't sustain change in the long run. Relentlessly means to stay focused on the end goal, gather people to their cause through conversations and listening, alter course where it makes sense, but make it clear that not trying is not an option. Stamina is a must, patience is a virtue to be leveraged liberally, and engagement will need to be early and often.

3. **PROJECT AND CHANGE MANAGERS**: the people charged with managing the change implementation. They may be project managers, change practitioners, functional leads, implementation partners, or others. Their role is to manage the moving parts, inform other parties of what is happening, and keep the change moving forward. They may not be people managers and may not even be directly impacted by the change. Some will bring expertise in making change happen, others will bring technical expertise needed for the change. It is important for the project and change managers to understand the big picture and the context in which the change is being implemented, so they can empathize with those who are impacted by the change. I've worked in organizations where the project managers are strictly focused on planning and tracking. I believe that project managers and those on the change project team need to understand the implications for the business and its people. Project teams play a

pivotal role in connecting the dots across deliverables and projects. They see all the pieces that are in play, and therefore need a broad understanding of the change initiatives.

The project team also plays an important role in engaging with the sponsors — through steering committees or one-on-one meetings. Outputs from planning and managing conversations should be discussed with the sponsors to keep them informed, seek decisions, highlight risks and solutions. Conversations with sponsors are also an opportunity for the project team to continually understand the sponsors' concerns, wishes, and expectations for the change.

4. **LEADERS**: those who lead the people in the organization or who are the face to external stakeholders such as customers, suppliers, or regulators. They are the first line of defense for questions from their teams or stakeholders and are also impacted by the change themselves. They fall into the tricky situation of having to lead the change without all the answers. See the section about Being a Successful Leader During Change on page xxi for more insight.

5. **TEAMS**: teams may be the sponsor group, the implementation team, impacted functions, or leadership teams; they may be permanent teams or temporary teams assembled during the change effort. Aligning teams around common goals and agreed-upon processes to move forward will enable a successful change. Teamwork is paramount during change, thus conversations among teams are needed to minimize team dysfunction and maximize effectiveness. I'm not specifically covering team alignment conversations in this book, but the AIM Changing Conversations will help teams function better during change. Also, see Appendix C for questions for your teams to consider.

6. **CHANGE CHAMPIONS**: these are the early adopters, super users, pilot leaders, experts and coaches; spreading their knowledge, excitement, and support throughout the organization to promote and build momentum for the change. Champions are the 'un-titled' leaders during change. They are often chosen from different groups at different levels in the organization, enabling

them to gather information about issues, risks, challenges, and benefits from a wide range of employees and to influence the progress of the change. Building a network of champions can be a pivotal strategy in implementing change. Conversations with this group are key to ensure alignment on messaging, gathering the feedback they hear on the ground, and continually improving their skills to lead change on the front lines. They may be involved in both Planning and Managing Conversations and Engagement Conversations. For ideas on how to set up your Champion Network, download the Five Steps to Build the Best Change Champion Network guide at www.actionimpactmovement.com/resources

> Bring others into the fight to do change right.

7. **EMPLOYEES**: all of the above roles are also employees of the organization, even leaders are employees first. Bringing those who make your business work everyday on board with the change takes ongoing effort. You need to bring them along the ABC Transition Roadmap™ and help them understand, believe, and take action. This is your largest group of people, and each one will have a unique perspective on the change. Conversations will happen in large groups, small groups, cross-functional groups, and one-on-one at various stages and with varying outcomes. You may have some employees who are not used to participating in facilitated group conversations, give them time to warm up through icebreaking activities or casual conversation. I led a group of utilities operators through a conversation about the changes to their team, this group was not used to being in a room all together and talking about their feelings and reactions! It took them a few minutes, but they eventually opened up to each other. Some gave silly answers, because they were uncomfortable, but most walked away feeling better about the changes and the direction the team was going.

8. **CUSTOMERS**: ultimately whatever you are changing will impact your customers. Hopefully to make their experience better. But depending on the change, maybe not. Engaging customers in conversation at the right time with the right information is an important part of the change. When focused on making change in our organizations we sometimes forget about our customers to the point of not serving them as well as we should.

   Depending on the change, you may need to bring them along the journey as well — are you making big changes to the way they receive service from your organization? Do they have ideas on how to make your organization better? When we consider why we are making change in the first place it can often be because of customer feedback. I worked with an organization whose customers were hospitals. We knew we needed to make process improvements, so we visited the hospitals and talked to decision makers, administrators, and most importantly, we talked to the staff who used the products and services every day. We got some great ideas for things we could do differently that we hadn't thought about before. That prompted us to implement even more changes to make it easier for our customers to receive and use our products. AIM Changing Conversations are a good opportunity to connect with customers for input and to help them transition through your change as well. See Appendix C for more questions to consider before engaging with customers.

9. **OTHER EXTERNAL STAKEHOLDERS**: your organization may have oversight or regulatory bodies. You may have associations or partners who have a vested interest in the workings and results of your organization. Based on the changes you are making you may need to have conversations with external stakeholders.

One More Time with Feeling

Three sets of conversations fill the following pages,

Ideas to self-reflect, to plan, and engage,

This chapter was used to set the stage,

If you need to do something, more, better, or different,

Then in conversation you will need to be,

Employees and clients, teams, champs, and sponsors,

One-on-one or in groups of many,

Leaders and managers and of course yourself too,

You know what to discuss and also with whom,

Up next are the questions, in part number three,

Then over to you to lead change and succeed!

PART THREE

AIM Changing Conversations: The Details and Questions

One last thing before you delve into the conversations!

Let's have a quick chat before we continue. There was a lot of information in those first two parts. All good stuff to know, but this is where the real fun begins. If, like me, you find facilitating great conversations, learning about others, and helping people move forward, fun! And if not, you'll at least be prepared and might eventually find it fun when you see how impactful conversations can be.

In Part Three I'm going to dive into the details of the 20 AIM Changing Conversations. For each conversation I'll provide some background, the purpose, the key questions to ask to get to the heart of the discussion, and next steps to take. Use the Conversation Planner from Chapter Five to prepare for your specific conversations. There is a blank template in Appendix A, or download a template at www.actionimpactmovement.com/resources

Take what you need from these conversation outlines. Use them as a starting point for leading change. Combine conversations or add your own questions — see Appendix C for more question ideas. Review the conversations and reference them again and again — *one more time with feeling.*

You may have guessed by now that I'm passionate about teaching and coaching others to lead change with confidence. I've provided instructions for each conversation but if you'd like additional support or coaching, visit my website for resources, or email me and we can start our conversation.

Happy conversing!

Jen
jen@actionimpactmovement.com

P.S. Would you provide an online review? Reviews help spread the word to more people about how they too can lead AIM Changing Conversations and implement change successfully. I'd love it if you would take a moment to provide an online review of this book. Thanks!

The 20 AIM Changing Conversations

Self-Reflection Conversations	Purpose
1. The Personality Preferences Conversation	Reflect on your personal preferences and how they may impact your approach to leading and accepting change.
2. The Personal Change Journey Conversation	Reflect on past experiences to uncover your approach to dealing with change and transition.
3. The Prepare Yourself to Lead Change Conversation	Develop your personal ABC Transition Roadmap™ to prepare to lead change.

Planning and Managing Conversations	Purpose
1. The Why Conversation	Identify the compelling reason(s) to make change now.
2. The What, When, and How Conversation	Decide what changes to make, then when, and how the changes will be implemented.
3. The Situation Conversation	Assess the magnitude of the change and the readiness of the organization to implement the change as input into project, change, and communication plans.
4. The Stakeholder Conversation	Identify all stakeholders in the change, what they need to do differently, why they might resist, and how to manage the resistance.
5. The Coordinate Your Asks Conversation	Identify activities across the organization and prioritize what you will ask of people during the change.
6. The Communication Planning Conversation	Develop a communication strategy.
7. The Performance Conversation	Identify the knowledge, skills, and behavior gaps between the old way and the new way, then create development plans to close the gaps. Align performance measures and rewards and recognition programs to reinforce the new structure and expectations.
8. The Status and Progress Conversation	Manage the activities, issues, and decisions involved in implementing the change, alter course as needed, and keep key stakeholders informed.
9. The Results Conversation	Assess the outcomes of the change to determine if desired results are being achieved.

Engagement Conversations	Purpose
1. The Debrief Conversation	Gauge what people have heard and understood about the announced changes.
2. The Impact Conversation	Identify the impact of changes on people and what they perceive they will lose and/or gain from the change.
3. The Change Track Record Conversation	Acknowledge the past and identify the actions to bring forward that have worked in past changes and avoid the things that didn't work.
	Identify the current structure, processes, or activities that will enable the change and those that will hinder the advancement of the change.
4. The Stop, Start, Continue Conversation	Identify priorities to create capacity to implement the change.
	Create ownership of ideas and solutions to realize the change.
5. The Coaching Conversation	Provide feedback and reflection opportunities to acknowledge and improve on performance needed to execute the change.
6. The Are You on Board? Conversation	Determine a path forward with those people who seem unwilling to change.
7. The Lessons Learned Conversation	Identify what's working and what's not with the change and adapt as needed.
8. The Celebration and Thank You Conversation	Celebrate wins during the change process and thank people for their efforts.

Self-Reflection Conversations

7

BY THIS POINT hopefully we all agree that for an organization to achieve the desired results of a change each individual needs to move through the ABC Transition Roadmap™ to commit to the change. You will have conversations with many people during this change journey, and the first conversations are with yourself — to reflect on your reactions, prepare, and decide how you will show up and lead during change. In this chapter, we're going to take a little pit stop on our road trip and pause to take in a key sightseeing attraction: you.

What Influences our Acceptance of Change?

Each person's perception and ultimate acceptance of change is based on their personality, their situation, their past experience, their values, and the choices they make. Our perception determines how we see the world — how we interpret new information, what conclusions we draw, and ultimately how we behave. Recall that people will transition and reach the new beginning stage of change at different rates based on their:

ROLE IN THE CHANGE: those who plan or instigate the change will transition first. These are generally the sponsors, the senior leaders who crafted the change. The rest of the employees (from leaders to managers to staff) will take longer to transition based on when they become aware of the change and their level of involvement in the change. In our marathon analogy, the employees are at the starting line of awareness when the sponsors are nearing the finish line of commitment.

EXTENT OF IMPACT FROM THE CHANGE: transition speed will depend on the timing of the change and the magnitude of change introduced. Those who implement the change first will start their transition first. This is often seen in 'phased rollouts' where a new process or platform is deployed to different groups over a period of time. Transition speed also depends on the magnitude of change required. In my 'SunHere and SandThere' example from Chapter Four, the new platform was an upgrade for SunHere, and even though both groups implemented the platform at the same time, it was easier and faster for SunHere to transition because they were already familiar with the platform.

PERSONALITY TYPE: your personality type and style preferences influence your readiness and acceptance of change. We'll use one model below to examine reactions to change based on personality type.

Ready to Start Your Self-Reflection Sightseeing?

I realize self-reflection is not everybody's idea of a good time. However, by answering the questions in the following conversations, you will gain insight into your personal reactions and readiness for change, and perhaps even have a couple of 'ah-ha' moments. As a coach, I know the value of 'ah-ha' moments, they are where personal transformation begins.

Self-Reflection Conversations	Purpose
1. The Personality Preferences Conversation	Reflect on your personal preferences and how they may impact your approach to leading and accepting change.
2. The Personal Change Journey Conversation	Reflect on past experiences to uncover your approach to dealing with change and transition.
3. The Prepare Yourself to Lead Change Conversation	Develop your personal ABC Transition Roadmap™ to prepare to lead change.

1. The Personality Preferences Conversation

Personal reactions to change are based on many things including personality preferences. Understanding your personality preferences is one method of building your self-awareness. Self-awareness and self-reflection are necessary ingredients for growth and learning and moving through transition. One way to understand your preferences is through personality assessments. Personality assessments are not meant to stereotype people or provide excuses for not being able to do something. They are an awareness-building tool to promote better understanding of yourself and others.

Using the Myers-Briggs Type Indicator (MBTI®), developed by Isabel Briggs Myers and Katherine Briggs, (based on the theory of personality type by Swiss psychiatrist Carl Jung), we'll examine tendencies related to change. Your Myers-Briggs type may impact your reactions as you move through the stages of transition. Some personality types may engage more readily with a change, while others may be more hesitant.

Myers-Briggs Type Indicator Preferences Characteristics

The MBTI® provides insight into your preferences in four areas:

- What gives you energy (extraversion vs. introversion)
- How you take in information (sensing vs. intuition)
- How you make decisions (thinking vs. feeling)
- Your approach to life (judging vs. perceiving)

Use the following type characteristics to consider your preferences. *(Myers, I.B. (2015). Introduction to Myers-Briggs® Type: A guide for understanding your results on the MBTI® assessment (7th edition; L.K. Kirby. Ed. & K.D. Myers, Ed.). The Myers-Briggs Company. (Original work published 1998)*

What gives you energy?

EXTRAVERSION (E)	INTROVERSION (I)
People with a preference for Extraversion are energized through contact with other people or through engaging in activities. Characteristics include:	People with a preference for Introversion are energized through ideas, quiet times, or solitude. Characteristics include:
▪ Attuned to external environment	▪ Drawn to their inner world
▪ Prefer to communicate by talking	▪ Prefer to communicate in writing
▪ Work out ideas by talking them through	▪ Work out ideas by reflecting on them
▪ Learn best by doing or discussing	▪ Learn best by reflection, mental 'practice'
▪ Have broad interests	▪ Focus in-depth on their interests
▪ Sociable and expressive	▪ Private and contained
▪ Readily take initiative in work and relationships as this is their opportunity to engage with the outside world	▪ Take initiative when the situation is very important to them, because it takes more energy to engage with the outside world

Circle the preference that best describes you — Extraversion (E) or Introversion (I)

82

How do you take in information?

SENSING (S)	INTUITION (N)
People with a preference for Sensing gather information through what they perceive through the five senses: seeing, hearing, touching, smelling, and tasting. Characteristics include:	People with a preference for Intuition gather information through what might be described as the sixth sense — the unseen world of meanings, inferences, hunches, insights and connections. Characteristics include:
• Oriented to present realities	• Oriented to future possibilities
• Take in information through the five senses	• Theoretical
• Factual, concrete and practical	• Imaginative and verbally creative
• Focus on what is real and actual	• Focus on patterns and meanings in data
• Observe and remember specifics	• Remember specifics when they relate to a pattern
• Build carefully and thoroughly toward conclusions (step-by-step)	• Move quickly to conclusions, follow hunches
• Understand ideas and theories through practical applications	• Want to clarify ideas and theories before putting them into practice
• Like perfecting established skills	• Like novelty and learning new skills
• Trust experience	• Trust inspiration

Circle the preference that best describes you — Sensing (S) or Intuition (N)

How do you make decisions?

THINKING (T)	FEELING (F)
People with a preference for Thinking prefer making decisions based on impartial criteria — cause-effect, reasoning, constant principles or truths, and logic. Characteristics include:	People with a preference for Feeling prefer to make decisions based on values, person-centered criteria, and creating harmony. Characteristics include:
• Analytical	• Empathetic and compassionate
• Use cause-and-effect reasoning	• Guided by personal values and individual needs
• Solve problems with logic	• Assess impact of decisions on people
• Strive for an objective standard of truth and justice	• Consider subjective criteria
• Reasonable	• Strive for harmony & positive interactions
• Can be 'tough-minded'	• May appear 'tender-hearted'
• Fair — want everyone treated equally	• Fair — want everyone to be treated as an individual

Circle the preference that best describes you — Thinking (T) or Feeling (F)

How do you approach life? How do you deal with the outer world?

JUDGING (J)	PERCEIVING (P)
People with a preference for Judging want to live an orderly life, with goals and structure, making decisions so they can move on. Characteristics include:	People with a preference for Perceiving want to live a spontaneous life with flexibility, staying open to new information and possibilities. Characteristics include:

- Scheduled

- Organize their lives and like things to be settled

- Systematic

- Methodical and like control

- Make short-term and long-term plans

- Like to have things decided

- Set goals and close things off

- Try to avoid last-minute stresses

- Spontaneous

- Flexible and casual

- Let life happen

- Open-ended, seek options

- Adapt, change course

- Like things loose and open to change

- Feel energized by last-minute pressures

Circle the preference that best describes you — Judging (J) or Perceiving (P)

To complete the full MBTI® assessment and receive your type report, visit www.actionimpactmovement.com/resources

Common responses to change based on Myers-Briggs Type

Are you someone who looks forward to change? Or someone who prefers things to stay the same. Change takes effort — energy, information gathering, decision making, and making sense of what is happening. Knowing your personality preferences provides insight into how you may react to the effort needed to change. Outlined below are some common responses to change based on the first two letters of your Myers-Briggs type (adapted from *MBTI® Optimizing Team Performance Program*, Second Edition, 2011 by Patrick L. Kerwin).

INTROVERSION / SENSING (IS): these people want to know the reason for the change (why) and the impact on their role. They like to have complete information about the change. Once they understand the reason for the change and what is happening, they will usually get on board and no longer resist the change.

EXTROVERSION / SENSING (ES): these people focus on practicality. Once they understand what the change is, if they believe it to be practical, they will not likely resist and will get on board quickly to support and take action for the change. They can move to new beginnings quickly. However, if the change seems impractical in their view, they may provide more resistance.

INTROVERSION / INTUITION (IN): these people want to understand the big picture and direction of the change. They will want time to think about and process the change and its impacts. Resistance rears its head if the change contradicts something that is very important to them or one of their values.

EXTROVERSION / INTUITION (EN): these people also want to understand the big picture and then talk with others about the change to 'process out loud'. They are likely to suggest further changes along the lines of, "well, since we're changing, let's make *this* change as well…"

In summary, understanding your personality preferences and recognizing how you respond to change helps you recognize how others may respond to change. Some people thrive in change — they love the new and novel — while others like steady state. My dad loves getting the latest technology gadget while my father-in-law still has a stand-alone answering machine.

The Personality
Preferences Conversation

Self-Reflection
Conversation 1

PURPOSE

Reflect on your personality preferences and how they may impact your approach to leading and accepting change.

QUESTIONS

1. Based on the definitions in the four MBTI® charts above, what is your estimated Myers-Briggs type? _ _ _ _ (write your selected letters in order, e.g., ISTJ)

2. Looking at the first two letters of your estimated type, review the common responses to change based on MBTI® type on the previous page. Which descriptions resonate with you?

3. Reflecting on your past change experiences, how did your personality preferences influence your reactions and actions?

4. What will you keep in mind about personality preferences when leading others through change?

2. The Personal Change Journey Conversation

Your past experience with change has a large impact on how willing you are to make new changes. If a previous change ended badly (e.g., termination, loads of extra work) you won't be keen to go through that again. On the flip side, a positive outcome from a change shows you what is possible and you'll be more inclined to try the next change.

Change is a series of conversations. Change is also a series of choices. These choices lead to decisions. Decisions to take action, take no action, do something different, or continue to do things the same way you have always done them — *one more time with feeling*. You make decisions every hour of every day. Various internet sources state that we make over 35,000 decisions per day! And, as we saw in the Myers-Briggs section above, we have a preferred way of making decisions. So how we make even the smallest of decisions (e.g., what to wear, what to eat) is similar to the way we make bigger decisions (e.g., to move across the country, to change jobs, or to accept the change being imposed at work, embrace it, and move forward).

Our choices are also influenced by our values. What do you value most? Do you know what each person impacted by the change values most? Least? Of course not. It's impossible to know everyone's values, but we can all agree that change which aligns to our values is easier for us to buy into. Leaders must acknowledge that people's values will be impacted by the change. During change, your values show up first in your fears and in the opportunities you see before you. Something that you fear you will lose is likely linked to something you value. If you value strong relationships and those are now threatened by a re-organization, you may have a hard time accepting the change. On the flip side, if you value new challenges and meeting new people, a change that requires you to work on a cutting-edge system with a new team may be a chance that you jump at without hesitation.

In this conversation, you'll examine your past experiences with change, the choices you made, and whether the change aligned (or didn't) to your values. From there you can draw conclusions and see patterns in how you react to change.

The Personal Change Journey Conversation

Self-Reflection Conversation 2

PURPOSE

Reflect on past experiences to uncover your approach to dealing with change and transition.

QUESTIONS

Identify two different changes you have experienced — at work (e.g., job change, promotion, new system or process) or in your personal life (e.g., exercise routine, diet, relationships). You may consider one that you chose (e.g., to move to a new city) and one that was imposed on you (e.g., new technology or reorganization at work).

Document your responses to the questions in the chart on the following page, then consider:

- What patterns emerged about how you reacted to and transitioned through change?

- How did your responses differ (or not) between the chosen and imposed changes?

- What insights will you take into the next change you experience?

Question	Change 1	Change 2
1. What prompted the change?		
2. What were your fears about the change?		
3. What did you perceive you might lose?		
4. What opportunities did the change represent (i.e., what were you hoping was going to be better because of the change, what did you perceive you might gain)?		
5. How did you experience the seven dynamics of change? i. What was awkward or uncomfortable? ii. What did you have to give up? iii. Did you feel all alone? iv. What other changes were also happening, did it feel like too much at once? v. When were you ready for the change (i.e., right away or it took some time to buy in)? vi. Were you concerned about not enough resources (e.g., time, money, support)? vii. Did you revert back the old way of doing things? If not, what compelled you to stay changed?		
6. Thinking about your values, how did the changes align to or contradict your values? How did your values influence your acceptance of the change?		
7. What was most challenging during the transition period for you?		
8. Did you resist the change? How did you resist (i.e., what did you do or say)?		
9. Did you ultimately commit to the change? What caused you to commit?		
10. What was the result of the change? Did you perceive the result to be positive or negative?		

Don't forget to consider these questions based on your responses above:

- What patterns emerged about how you reacted to and transitioned through change?

- How did your responses differ (or not) between the chosen and imposed changes?

- What insights will you take into the next change you experience?

Our success or failure with past change influences our perception and acceptance of future change. As the saying goes, those who are once bitten are twice shy. Not wanting to repeat painful situations is a strong deterrent to entering into another change situation. The possibility of the future has to be more compelling than the current status quo. When change comes your way next — either chosen or imposed — consider how your past experiences will influence you to either run towards it or back away slowly.

3. The Prepare Yourself to Lead Change Conversation

How will you lead the next change? And every change after that? Some will be easier for you and some will be more challenging. As a leader, ask yourself if you are ready to embrace the change or need more time, information, or support to drive forward. Are you ready to lead the change and set an example for others? This conversation is the opportunity for you to reflect on what you need, and will seek out, to support your own transition and to prepare to lead others through change.

The Prepare Yourself to Lead Change Conversation

Self-Reflection Conversation 3

PURPOSE

Develop your personal ABC Transition Roadmap™ to prepare to lead change.

QUESTIONS

Taking into consideration your MBTI® preferences and your responses to past changes, it's time to decide how you will lead future changes — changes you choose, and changes imposed on you. Using the ABC Transition Roadmap™, answer the following questions to build your personal roadmap through change:

1. **AWARENESS**: How will I build my awareness of the change? What information will I want (e.g., big picture, details, etc.)?

2. **BUY-IN**: What will enable me to buy into the change? What impacts will I want to know about (e.g., to me, to my team, etc.)?

3. **BELIEF**: What will make me believe that the change is possible (e.g., facts, research, demonstrations, trying it out myself, testimonials from those I trust, etc.)?

4. **CAPABILITY**: How will I build my capability? How do I like to learn (e.g., reading, experiencing, lectures, etc.)?

5. **CAPACITY**: How will I create personal capacity to make the change? What work will I need to prioritize?

6. **COMMITMENT**: What will cause me to commit to the change?

7. **CONTINUE**: What support will I need to continue this change and make decisions in alignment with the new direction (e.g., coaching, mentors, connections, resources, etc.)?

The Team ABC Transition Roadmap™ — Using the same questions, you can build an ABC Transition Roadmap™ for your team or organization. For example, how will you build awareness among *the team*? What will compel *your team* to commit to the change? How will you create capacity for *your team or organization* to make the change? For more team questions, see Appendix C.

My ABC Transition Roadmap™ Journey to Become a Skier

My transition to becoming a skier started with awareness. I was moving to the mountains and I was well aware that I would need to take up skiing if I wanted to spend time with my family during the winter. I had snowboarded for about eight years off and on, but as my husband liked to point out, "you're not getting any more courage on your snowboard, Jen." I reflected on my experience and decided it was time to take up skiing. I bought in, I wanted to try skiing, I purchased the gear, signed up for lessons and showed up on day one ready, though somewhat terrified!

Next up I had to *believe* that I could become a competent skier. Without belief in that change, it was not going to happen. Having others believe in me was a start — the ski instructors were clearly well-trained to stoke my confidence. And then there was the practice, I needed mileage, more time on the mountain, more practice and feedback to improve my skiing ability and my confidence. I created the capacity to improve my capability, carving out 50 days of skiing my first year. Throughout the following three years I participated in over 40 ski lessons, and the most important lesson I learned is that you have to commit. When you start down a run you have to be all in. Being only half-committed greatly raises your chances of being trolleyed down the mountain in a stretcher sled behind a ski patroller. Remember the conversation with myself while standing at the top of never-skied-by-me run I mentioned previously? Those are what convinced me to commit. Not fully committing to a change takes a lot of extra energy — you end up wearing two hats — the old one and the new one and they often don't complement each other. Getting yourself over the finish line of commitment and continuing the change is not always easy but staying on the fence and not committing is an uncomfortable place to be.

I have successfully made the transition to become a skier, and to remain a competent skier I continue to take lessons and go up the mountain as often as possible to practice, as there are always ski runs that I can learn to do better, faster and with more finesse.

So, have the conversations with yourself that get you to the point of being all-in to commit to and lead change.

Side Conversations to Have with Yourself

As my mom says, "talking to myself keeps me sane", so here are a few other conversations to have with yourself as you lead through change.

1. **LET IT GO**: Elsa from Disney's *Frozen* said it best. What do you need to let go of? What can you let go of? What is holding you back? A sense of responsibility, of keeping things the same, of not rocking the boat? You have long-held beliefs that may not be serving you well anymore, and in order to lead others through change, you need to make some changes first. Let it go!

2. **OFF THE LIST**: leading change takes time and effort so something will have to give. Truly assess what you can delegate or simply stop doing. What is your top 10 list (i.e., the things that you do all the time, your top priorities)? What are numbers 8, 9, and 10 on that list? It's time to delegate those. Those items will be a great stretch learning opportunity for someone else. Giving them away will free up your time to focus on other things that matter for the change.

3. **RESILIENCE 101**: resilience is the ability to bounce back. To be able to bounce back you need to take care of yourself. For real. You are no good to anyone in a stressed-out, strung-out state. Recognize when you are in that state (or ideally before you get there) and do something to change it. In some of my early consulting days, long before there was so much attention on self-care and mental health, we worked a ridiculous number of hours in a week. Let me restate that, we were at the office or the client site for a ridiculous number of hours in a week. We were not productive the whole time, we were putting in 'face time' but not always adding value. Refocus your efforts on adding value versus just being there. You have time for whatever you make time for so make time to recharge and manage your energy and you'll add a lot more value when you are there. What activities help you build your resilience? Exercise, reading, meditation, social activities, family time? How will you make time for those?

4. **CONTINUOUS LEARNING**: studies reveal that learning new things can keep your brain healthier, longer. Continuous learning will also help build a learning culture in your organization — this is how you stay relevant, 'ahead of the curve', and remain nimble to react to changes that might sneak up on you, or more importantly, how you can be proactive so that very few changes can sneak up on you! If the people in your organization stagnate and stop learning, you will be passed by competitors. How will you continue to learn and set an example for others? What do you want to learn next?

Where to Next?

From here we'll move on to Planning and Managing Conversations. If you love to be organized and make plans, you're going to the right place. If you don't love to be organized but know you need to, you're also going to the right place. If you're considering making changes in your team or organization and want to know where to start, the next chapter is definitely the right place for you. Let's go!

One More Time With Feeling

That pit stop was intense, the mirror focused on you,

To discover your type preferences and personal reactions too,

Next up we start planning the why, what, and how,

To organize our change efforts, let's get started right now!

Planning and Managing Conversations

8

THESE CONVERSATIONS ARE the ones to use to decide, organize, plan, and manage change initiatives. Those instigating the change — who generally become the ultimate sponsors — spend many hours, weeks, or months planning changes.

They will have multiple Why Conversations and What, When, and How Conversations just to get to the point of *deciding* that they want change to happen. Working through these conversations helps them on their ABC Transition Roadmap™ journey through change. As they discuss, debate, and decide why and what to change, they develop their awareness, they buy in and believe the change is possible, and they build their commitment to the change.

The project and change managers — those charged with managing implementation — also participate in a whole host of conversations to assess impacts, identify possible resistance, plan needed training and coaching, develop the communication strategy, and organize many other actions required for the change effort. All of these are important conversations to plan and manage change effectively.

Planning and Managing Conversations	Purpose
1. The Why Conversation	Identify the compelling reason(s) to make change now.
2. The What, When, and How Conversation	Decide what changes to make, then when, and how the changes will be implemented.
3. The Situation Conversation	Assess the magnitude of the change and the readiness of the organization to implement the change as input into project, change, and communication plans.
4. The Stakeholder Conversation	Identify all stakeholders in the change, what they need to do differently, why they might resist, and how to manage the resistance.
5. The Coordinate Your Asks Conversation	Identify activities across the organization and prioritize what you will ask of people during the change.
6. The Communication Planning Conversation	Develop a communication strategy.
7. The Performance Conversation	Identify the knowledge, skills, and behavior gaps between the old way and the new way, then create development plans to close the gaps. Align performance measures and rewards and recognition programs to reinforce the new structure and expectations.
8. The Status and Progress Conversation	Manage the activities, issues, and decisions involved in implementing the change, alter course as needed, and keep key stakeholders informed.
9. The Results Conversation	Assess the outcomes of the change to determine if desired results are being achieved.

1. The Why Conversation

Why are we changing? Change is often a reaction to external forces — competition, technology changes, regulation, legislation, availability of resources, or industry trends. The reason for change may be based on customer feedback, external benchmarking, or best practice studies. Reaching agreement to change can take many conversations, part of which must include: why are we changing and why now?

It's important to look at the symptoms that are causing you to consider change. Is employee morale down, have sales stagnated, is the procurement process taking too long? You need to consider why these symptoms are appearing and ask what would be different if these trends were reversed? What would be better or different if morale were improved? What would be better if sales increased? Asking the 'what would be better or different?' question helps pinpoint why you want to change and the ultimate result you are seeking. The next question to ask is — how much of a difference will changing make? You need to know your primary objective — to increase sales? For what reason? To have more money to reinvest into new programs, equipment, or initiatives?

Also think about why you are changing — is it chosen or imposed? Chosen change is driven by the desire to take the organization in a new direction. Imposed change is driven by external forces, such as new legislation that requires change by a specified date. Knowing what instigated the change helps determine an approach to make the change successful. In the case of chosen change, you are considering *whether or not* to make a change. In the case of imposed change, you are deciding *how* you will make the change successfully (because the decision to change is a foregone conclusion).

Why change? It isn't just about setting strategy.

Answering the 'why change?' question is not just about setting strategy. There are loads of books and resources about how to develop a strategic plan. The essence of the Why Conversation is the start of the transition process. Wrestling the why questions to the ground (i.e., debating why to make a change, having input and the ability to question it) starts to build the buy-in, belief, and commitment of those involved in the conversation. It builds their conviction to support and lead the change.

An important complement to the why question is the success question: how will we know when we have been successful? I used to work with a leader who would say, "I'll know it when I see it." This was hard to measure and hard for people to achieve because they lacked a clear picture of the desired result. What will be gained by change and what will success look like are essential questions to ask.

Lastly, reaching consensus on the *reason* for the change and the desired results may be challenging, and that's okay. It's important for those deciding on and developing the change direction to debate, discuss, and understand the implications, the opportunities and the challenges of changing. Through these discussions they will go through the transition from old world to new world. Let's see this conversation in action.

Planning and Managing Conversation 1	The Why Conversation

PURPOSE

Identify the compelling reason(s) to make change now.

WHEN TO HAVE THE CONVERSATION

- As part of regular strategic planning sessions — continually scanning the internal and external environments to anticipate and react to forces that require change.
- As part of the decision process to undertake change, then on-going to confirm that you are still changing for the right reasons.

WHO'S INVOLVED

Senior leaders and those who will be sponsors of the change

BACKGROUND INFORMATION

Gather any research, expertise, or insights needed to decide on and create the compelling reason to change.

QUESTIONS

Considering change questions

- What is happening outside the organization that is driving us to consider change?
- What customer feedback is driving the need to change?
- What are our competitors doing?
- What are the forces creating pressure on our organization? Political, social, technological, economic, other?

Why change questions

- Why do we want to make change?
- Why do we want to make change now?
- What are the different results we want to achieve?
- What is our vision for the future of the organization?
- What will be better or different because of this change?
- What organizational values are driving this change?
- What will we gain by making changes?
- What is the logic behind the change?
- Why will this change be different than past changes?
- What are the benefits of changing?

Consequences of change questions

- What are the consequences of not changing?
- What might we lose by making changes?

Success of the change questions

- What will success look like?
- How much of a difference will changing make?
- How will we know when we have achieved success?
- What will be the indicators/measures of success or failure?

NEXT STEPS

- Summarize why you are making change and the desired results.
- Start to engage other leaders in the organization in conversations about the reasons why change is needed (even prior to knowing the what, when, and how).

2. The What, When, and How Conversation

Once you know why you want to change and the desired results, it's time to figure out what will change, when it will change, and how you will make it happen. You will have this conversation with different groups as you plan the steps and actions for implementation.

What will change?

I joined an insurance company going through massive organizational change. On my second day I was invited to a project meeting. There were at least 30 people in the room and the leaders were talking about the new technology that was going to be implemented: a customer relationship management system for the insurance agents to track their sales funnel, document their contacts, and report on their wins and losses.

The whole discussion centered around the technology and the next steps for implementation. At the end of the meeting someone asked me what I thought. My first response was, "the technology seems to be driving the process — you've decided on the technology solution but I'm not sure you know the problem you are trying to fix with it just yet."

I had learned from many hours of drawing 'as-is' and 'to-be' process maps that people need to understand what is happening now and then they can look at what could be different with the aid of technology or process changes.

Technology should not drive process.

Nowadays, it feels like technology is in the driver's seat, a new app or platform hits the scene and how we do things changes (e.g., online ordering, social media, etc.), but *first* there was the thinking about what was wrong with the current way of doing things or the current results. Then there was the decision about what could be different. Note: this is not a 'requirements document' where you write down all the possible things you need technology to do. This is looking at your current processes — how do we work now and what is the result that is produced from the way we currently do things?

In the situation of the insurance company above, they had decided on the technology solution before they had a full understanding of the current sales process and how the technology would impact it. The initial launch was lackluster. The insurance agents, many of whom had worked for the company for years, were accustomed to meeting with their clients in their homes or coffee shops and they took notes on paper or the proverbial 'back of the napkin'. They had never used laptops in front of their clients nor documented the vast amount of information now required for the new platform. There was a large gap between the 'as-is' and the 'to-be' processes that had not been addressed.

It was time to take a step back. A sales process document was developed with input from the current sales force. It was huge, many pages of what happened at each stage of the process. Not exciting reading, but definitely the key to figuring out what had to change to achieve the desired business results and how the technology would support the goals.

So, the first step in the What, When, and How Conversation is this: dig into how activities happen now and the results accomplished by those activities, then, based on the new results you desire, identify what needs to change — activities, performance levels, processes, technology, behaviors, or people.

It may be that you have to implement a new system because the old one is no longer supported. Fair enough. But first, have a look at the results the current system or process is providing. I worked in a learning team where we had to replace the evaluation platform because the old one was being decommissioned. It was a big project to look at different vendors, compare requirements and costs, and decide the path forward.

At one point the team stepped back and asked themselves what they wanted the future of measurement and evaluation to be. Instead of focusing on a current specifications comparison, they developed their process goals — what do we want to evaluate, what do we want to demonstrate with a measurement strategy, how many levels of measurement do we want in the future and why. Then they were in a better position to decide on the technology that would best support their desired business state. And the technology didn't drive the decision making.

Many times I've seen the stars buyers get in their eyes when all the bells and whistles are described by the vendor — all the reports, the slicing and dicing, the different ways you can use their platform. Buyers become focused on the flashy technology and on what they might lose if they don't buy the five-star version of the platform — remember our discussions about focusing on losses first during change in Chapter Two? In my experience organizations use only a fraction of the functionality of the five-star technology platform, therefore the three-star version is often adequate to achieve your business goals.

Decide what needs to change by looking at the different business results you want.

For example, if you want sales revenue to increase to $4 million and your current sales revenue is $3 million, you need to improve by at least $1 million (assuming no attrition of other sales occurs). Next you look at the performance that is creating that current $3 million in sales revenue. What are people doing to earn the current sales revenue? What do they need to do more, better or different to earn an extra $1 million in sales revenue? What processes need to be altered to enable them to improve? What skills do they need to change? What performance measures need to be different to change behavior?

And lastly, consider what is not changing. What will remain the same? I worked with a large professional services firm implementing a new technology platform. It was the largest change to hit the practice in years as they were changing both methodology and technology. Part of the messaging was what was *not* changing — relationship skills, sound judgment, knowledge of their clients — these skills would still be needed in the new world. Knowing this helped lower the anxiety levels of those impacted by the changes.

When will the change happen?

Timing is everything, as the saying goes. Depending on what must change, the timing of a change may not be optimal, for example, meeting regulation or external deadlines regardless of your business cycle. Where possible, consider your business cycle and plan changes for slower periods. A plant I worked at had many outdoor facilities, which made upgrade projects challenging to complete in the cold and snowy winter months. Major projects were scheduled for the spring, between winter and the busy summer season.

The 'go-live' date of the tour operator I worked with, who implemented a new reservations system, was delayed and we ended up launching in the middle of hurricane season. I'll never forget the morning we 'flipped the switch' on the new system, with fingers crossed for no travel glitches. There were hurricanes threatening many of the company's sunny tourist destinations. It was not an ideal launch date and it took a number of all-nighters to cross that finish line, but in the end all travelers got where they needed to be and home again.

Assess the on-going operational activities of your organization and the amount of work needed to make the changes. Then decide the ideal timing for your change, and a contingency date. I've worked on enough systems implementations to know that the best laid plans of mice and men often go awry, as adapted from a Robert Burns poem and an ode to my grade five teacher who was Scottish. Missing dates can put other projects or daily operations in jeopardy, so plan accordingly.

How will you make the change?

The Fairy Godmother (I recently watched all the *Disney Descendants* movies with my kids) may not be available to bibbity-bobbity-boo your change into reality, so you'll have to make it happen without magic. How to make the change is also dependent on what the change is. Do you have the skills to make the changes in-house? Do you have the time and capacity to make the changes in-house? Do you have the desire, money, and effort required to hire external resources? Will you pilot or test the changes before launching across the entire organization? Will a group of change champions be needed to support the new way?

How the changes are made will depend on the capacity and capability of your people, and of course the timing and costs. When external consultants are brought in the work can usually be done faster but, if internal people are not involved in the project they don't benefit from learning as part of the change team.

The acceptance of change is also impacted by how the change is made. If people are handed a final product without ever having had input or involvement, their acceptance and ability to act in the new way will be slower. However, involving internal people in making the change will mean that something else will have to give in their workload, or you risk overloading your people. You must find the right balance of timing and resources to make change happen.

Lastly, you need to consider how you will sustain the change over time. This includes creating documentation (e.g., process and procedure manuals), removing old content from files, discarding artifacts (e.g., items with previous branding or logos), disposal of any hardware or equipment, and deleting platforms or apps that will no longer be used. Sustaining the change also includes reinforcement of skills and behaviors which is outlined in the Performance Conversation below.

You will not have all the answers the first time you have the What, When, and How Conversation. Document as much information as possible then continue to have the conversation to build out your plans.

The What, When, and How Conversation

Planning and Managing Conversation 2

PURPOSE

Decide what changes to make, then when, and how the changes will be implemented.

WHO'S INVOLVED

- Senior leaders and those who will be the sponsors of the change
- Others with insight into the changes required (e.g., IT for technology changes, HR for people/structure changes, Business Analysts for process changes, leaders and employees with knowledge of the impacted processes, systems, or tools, etc.)

QUESTIONS

What questions

- Business results and performance
  - What are our current business results?
  - What activities/performance/tools create our current results?
  - What are our desired business results?
  - What needs to change to achieve the desired results — people, processes, technology?
- What has to happen to achieve the vision?
- What is not changing?
- Customers
  - What do our customers need us to do differently?
  - What do we need to change to serve our customers better?
  - What other ways can we deliver our products or services to our customers and still realize the benefits of the change?
- What regulations, rules, or other external requirements do we need to comply with? What do we need to change to comply?

- What are the interdependencies of the changes (i.e., what impact will changes in one area of the organization have on another area)?
- Processes
  - What are the current processes in place? How will they change and why?
  - What processes need to be modified? Replaced? Eliminated?
  - What new processes need to be developed?
- People
  - What new skills or knowledge will be needed by current employees?
  - Will any skill sets or groups of people become redundant as a result of this change? Who, where, when?
- Structure
  - What changes will happen to roles, responsibilities, or authority?
  - What changes will happen to operating locations (e.g., open or close facilities, relocate people, relocate equipment or technology)?
  - What new governance models are needed?
- Technology and Systems
  - Will existing technology change and how will it change?
  - What new technology is being implemented?
  - What are the infrastructure requirements to enable the change (e.g., systems, hardware, licensing, number of users, etc.)?

When questions
- What does our business cycle look like (i.e, map out the on-going business events for the year)?
- When is the ideal time for changes to happen in our business cycle (e.g., slow periods, annual performance cycle, off-season manufacturing time, etc.)?
- What periods are 'non-negotiable' for changes to occur (e.g., busiest operating months)?
- Considering what changes are being made, when will they happen?
- What is the required sequence of change (i.e., what has to happen first, or before something else)?

- What is the pace of change (e.g., timing of new modules, timing of new equipment deliveries, etc.)?
- What is the fall-back or contingency date to implement the change?

How questions

- Who will lead the overall changes, different workstreams, and/or projects?
- What other projects need to be stopped or delayed in order to focus on this change?
- How will users/employees provide input into the changes? At what intervals/milestones?
- Is external expertise needed to make the changes?
- Do we have the skills to complete the changes in-house?
- Do we have the time and capacity to complete the changes in-house?
- Who will need to be involved to make the changes a reality?
- How will we recruit any new people needed?
- Will we pilot or test the change with a select group prior to a full rollout? If yes, how?
- Do we need a group of change champions to support the implementation? If yes, who are the right people and how will we recruit and train them?
- How will we maintain acceptable levels of customer service during the change?

How much questions

- How much will the changes cost?
- What is the budget for the changes, will it cover the expected costs?
- How is the change being funded?
- Is there a contingency fund?

How will the change be maintained questions

- What documentation is needed related to the change (e.g., new process and procedure manuals)?
- What needs to be removed because it's no longer needed in the new world (e.g., branded items, apps, platforms, hardware, equipment, files)?
- What else is needed to maintain the changes?

NEXT STEPS

- Create your project plans — involve those who will be managing the deliverables and implementation.

3. The Situation Conversation

The impact of change is different for each individual and each organization. Seemingly small changes, like the type of lids provided for coffee cups at cafes, could have a big impact on certain people. If the new lid requires two hands to affix or open, someone with one arm in a sling will have a hard time using it. Large changes like an entire workforce having to work from home may have a small impact on those who already regularly work from home. Hence, the situational nature of change needs to be accounted for. Changes impact people differently, at different paces, at different times and for different reasons.

Changes impact organizations differently as well. Once you have determined *why* the change is needed and the general direction for the *what, when, and how*, it's important to assess the organizational situation. In organizations, the following factors impact the degree of change effort required, the readiness of the organization to implement change, and the ultimate success of the change implementation:

MATURITY LEVEL: start-ups and early-stage entrepreneurial organizations with less infrastructure and fewer legacy systems and processes may be able to move faster than mature or growing organizations and thus require different change and transition strategies.

NUMBER OF PEOPLE AND PROCESSES AFFECTED: isolated impacts (i.e., a single business unit) may require less change effort and resources compared to an organization-wide change.

DEGREE OF BEHAVIOR CHANGE REQUIRED: the greater the departure from current behavior and skills, the greater the degree of change effort and resources required. The ultimate behavior change is when organizations are looking to change their culture.

CHANGE TRACK RECORD: past success or failure with change will impact change efforts going forward — either as an enabler or as an obstacle.

RESOURCES FOR CHANGE: availability of resources will impact the change efforts required — this includes both resources to support and enable the change (e.g., project team, leaders, change champions) and resources needed to successfully realize the benefits of the change (e.g., hiring more people to deliver on a new sales or service strategy).

Some organizations will undertake extensive readiness assessments and planning. The Situation Conversation will get the ball rolling to understand how change will impact your organization.

The Situation Conversation

Planning and Managing
Conversation 3

PURPOSE

Assess the magnitude of the change and the readiness of the organization to implement the change as input into project, change, and communication plans.

WHO'S INVOLVED

- Senior leaders and those who will be the sponsors of the change
- Others with insight into the changes required (e.g., IT for technology changes, HR for people/structure changes, Business Analysts for process changes, leaders and employees with knowledge of the impacted processes, systems, or tools, etc.)

QUESTIONS

Magnitude questions

- How many changes are being made simultaneously? Include all changes — operational (e.g., new hires), seasonal (e.g., switch over of operations from summer to winter), transformational (e.g., major system, process, or structure change).
- What is the maturity of the organization? How established are the processes and structures?
- How many different stakeholder groups will be involved to create this change (e.g., # of functions, external resources, etc.)?
- How many different stakeholder groups will be impacted by the change?
- To what to degree are the tasks and/or environment changing?
- How many people need to learn new skills/behaviors to achieve the change?
- What is the timeline to complete the change?

Readiness questions

- What is the degree of leadership agreement regarding the reason for change?
- What is the degree of leadership agreement on what is going to change?
- What is the leaders' level of buy-in and belief in the change?
- How many resources are allocated to assist with the change effort? Are they the 'right' resources?
- What is the organization's track record for successfully implementing change?

NEXT STEPS

Based on the results of the conversation:

- Determine the right pace of change, review the timing, create communication plans.
- Consider what Engagement Conversations will be needed and when.

4. The Stakeholder Conversation

Who is affected by the changes?

This is your chance to create a stakeholder map! Who are all the people affected by the change? Inside and outside your organization. The length of this list depends on the magnitude of your changes. The key is to group people together to make your list manageable. Each person affected will react differently based on their circumstances and situation, but grouping people together is a great starting point.

For example, if you are implementing a new technology platform for a consulting practice, obviously the whole practice is impacted. But you'd want to break that group down into smaller audiences; the partners and managers will be impacted differently than the staff and seniors. The support groups — IT, Human Resources, Risk Management, etc. will also be impacted differently but still have a part to play in the success of the rollout. Impact also depends on perspective. In this technology example, the new platform is the only platform the newly hired staff will have ever used — therefore they have nothing to 'unlearn', while it may be the third or fourth iteration for the partners or senior managers, meaning they need to unlearn old habits and change their thinking.

Mapping out different audiences helps you develop a picture of what will be needed to win people over to commit and continue the change.

The stakeholder conversation will happen many times as you gain more information about the change and observe the reactions of the different groups. Identifying what each audience will need to know or do to implement the changes will help pinpoint further conversations and communications required. To answer the questions in this conversation you need to understand what each audience does on a day-to-day basis. As you learn more about the new platform or the new way of working you will continue to add to your stakeholder map. You will also start to identify what benefits people might perceive with the change, and also why people might resist the change.

117

Review Chapter Three on Dealing with Resistance prior to this conversation and consider why people might resist (e.g., not aware, not able, not willing) as well as what they may perceive as losses or gains from the change. You may not have all the answers to these questions yet. This is your best guess for planning purposes. As you start to engage others in conversation you will gain more insight into these questions. Download a Stakeholder Map template at www.actionimpactmovement.com/resources

The Stakeholder Conversation

Planning and Managing Conversation 4

PURPOSE

Identify all stakeholders in the change, what they need to do differently, why they might resist, and how to manage the resistance.

WHO'S INVOLVED

Change project team and others with insight into the changes required (e.g., IT for technology changes, HR for people/structure changes, Business Analysts for process changes, leaders and employees with knowledge of the impacted processes, systems, or tools, etc.)

QUESTIONS

Who questions

- Who is impacted by the change?
- What groupings make sense — how are those impacted the same or different?

Impact questions — for each group consider:

- What will this group need to know in order to make the change?
- What will this group need to be able to do to make the change?
- What are the perceived benefits of the change for this group?
- Why might this group resist the change (e.g., not aware, not able, not willing, perceived losses)?
- What is this group's current level of understanding of the change (e.g., low, medium, high)?
- What is this group's current level of commitment to the change (e.g., against it, will allow it to happen, will help it happen, will make it happen)?
- What level of commitment is needed from this group?

119

Action questions

- What actions are needed to address possible resistance and enable this group to commit to the change?

NEXT STEPS

- Create your stakeholder map using the responses.
- Use this information to inform your communication and engagement plans.

5. The Coordinate Your Asks Conversation

I also call this the 'avoiding the raindrop effect' conversation. You want to prioritize and organize requests from different groups before you send them out to all your employees. How many times have you been on the receiving end of contradictory priorities from different groups? Or simply received too many emails and been overloaded with information requests and missed a deadline. Coordinating asks across groups is key during major change, and a great everyday practice if you can make it happen.

I worked with a leadership team who was rolling out a new strategy. There were strategic initiatives that needed to be acted upon. There were also the day-to-day activities to continue — performance reviews, reporting, training, etc. We gathered all the employee 'asks' from each function (e.g., when training had to be completed, when performance reviews were due, timing of employee surveys, when reporting deadlines occurred) and mapped them against our strategic project 'asks'. We did the work of coordinating and planning 'at head office', before landing the asks on the 'field' (employees). Therefore, it didn't feel like raindrops coming from all directions, but a thoughtful and organized approach. It also meant that employees didn't have to make the decision on which activity to prioritize, the leaders had done this for them.

Month in a Box

I use a template I call 'month in a box' to coordinate this information. A spreadsheet to map the type of initiatives, the impact on people, and the timing or due dates. The questions for this conversation cover the key areas to track on the template. When all groups feed into this process you can see how many actions employees are asked to do and by when. Sometimes it's hard to believe we get any work done in a day with all the requests coming from different groups!

Download the Month in a Box template at www.actionimpactmovement.com/resources

The goal of this conversation is to identify priorities and see the impact on people across the organization — when are initiatives landing on the employees, how many actions are they asked to take in a given timeframe? Mapping your initiatives against the day-to-day and cyclical work requirements will provide a better picture of any capacity concerns and the ability to shift requests to slower periods where possible.

The Coordinate Your Asks Conversation

> **Planning and Managing Conversation 5**

PURPOSE

Identify activities across the organization and prioritize what you will ask of people during the change.

WHO'S INVOLVED

- Change project team and others with insight into the changes required (e.g., IT for technology changes, HR for people/structure changes, Business Analysts for process changes, leaders and employees with knowledge of the impacted processes, systems, or tools, etc.)
- Representatives from each group to identify their asks of employees
- Communication professionals to help with messaging and coordinating

This is a conversation to have regularly across groups and the change team to assess the volume and timing of asks of employees.

QUESTIONS

General questions

- How will we ensure that this change initiative is not derailed because people are distracted by other projects?
- How will we ensure that employee groups most affected by the change are not overwhelmed?
- How are we balancing the pace of change needed with running our business?

Month in a box questions

Each question can be a column in a spreadsheet with the initiatives listed down the left side.

- What initiatives are happening over the next month (or longer term)? List and provide some details for understanding.
- What is the deadline for this initiative (e.g., training to be complete by X date or performance review done by X date)?
- What is the priority ranking for this initiative? Criteria might include:
  - High — must comply for regulatory reasons or has to be complete before another project can start.
  - Medium — important for ongoing business operations (e.g., performance reviews complete by X date to feed into bonus allocation decisions).
  - Low — no specific deadline (e.g., updating personal information for optional volunteer opportunities).
- Who/which group initiated the request?
- What business objective does the initiative support?
- What other initiatives does this one link to (if any)?
- Who's affected by the initiative (i.e., who has to do something)? List the audiences (consider aligning your audiences to those in your stakeholder map).
- What do those affected need to do (e.g., complete training, fill in forms, use a new platform, etc.)?
- How much time/effort will it take for people to do what's needed (e.g., attend 1.5 hour training, read new regulation, complete profile, etc.)?
- What is the cost for this initiative (e.g., course fee per participant, license fees, project costs, etc.)?
- What is the risk of not completing this initiative?
- Based on the overall picture of all initiatives for timeframe, is the initiative approved (yes/no) or deferred (to when)?

NEXT STEPS

- Download the Month in a Box template at www.actionimpactmovement.com/resources

- Map all strategic, operational, and change-related activities on a timeline, noting the audience impacted by each activity.

- In periods where people will be overwhelmed with tasks, consider what can be delayed, advanced, reduced, or removed.

6. The Communication Planning Conversation

Now that you have coordinated your asks, next you need to coordinate your messaging. Communication planning during change will be fluid. As the change changes, so will your communication plans, however, developing an overall strategy and guiding principles will help you manage communication throughout the change. Your communication strategy will include one-way tactics, for example, emails, presentations, handouts, and also two-way communication and feedback opportunities — conversations! The Engagement Conversations will give you ideas to build into your overall communication strategy.

Communication will raise awareness of the change, the first step in our ABC Transition Roadmap™. Overall, communication activities should:

1. Promote the change — what is happening, why, and when.

2. Demonstrate what will be different — start using new language, demonstrating new tools or processes.

3. Minimize resistance to and risk of rejection of the change — anticipating and answering questions as people seek understanding during times of change.

4. Minimize the rumor mill — when there is a lack of information people will inherently make up their own information in the form of speculation or rumors.

5. Build the knowledge base of key change champions — those who will support others through transition.

6. Demonstrate that you are leading the change — even though the change may be due to a crisis or necessity, it's important to show that you are leading it versus it is leading you.

People will pay attention when the content being communicated is relevant to them.

You may feel like you are constantly communicating — *one more time with feeling* — but until people believe the message is relevant to them, they will not pay a lot of attention. You want to communicate when you have something to say, but not so much that people stop listening and your communication becomes background noise. People have many priorities to focus on in a day — as we saw in our Coordinate Your Asks Conversation. Continue to communicate and eventually you will gain the attention of those who need to know or do something different. The first reason for resistance is lack of awareness, so keep communicating!

I received an email from the IT team once saying my computer was going to be shut off from the network in ten days. Yikes! I was leaving the next morning for a two-week vacation. I picked up the phone to start my first conversation about this change. The IT person told me I should have received several pop-up notices about this change but apparently those didn't work on my computer. Therefore, whoever sent the final warning email likely assumed I was ignoring the messages, when in fact I didn't even get them, I simply didn't know. The conversation resulted in action, I shipped my computer to the office for updating and by the time I returned from vacation it was back and my network connections were restored.

Crafting your communication plan starts with your key messages so that all communications are 'singing from the same song sheet'. The outputs of your Why Conversation will help you develop these messages. Repeating your key messages in multiple forums builds the new language of the change. Constantly hearing the same messages builds awareness and, based on how well your messages resonate with your people, will start to build buy-in and belief in the change. Having a few, impactful key messages that are repeated by leaders and project teams will help align all those working on the change, and, in turn, ensure those impacted by the change hear the same messages from all parties.

Recall our foray into the Myers-Briggs Type Indicator in Chapter Seven. When building your communication plan, consider the unique preferences of the different types:

- **EXTRAVERSION** – provide an opportunity to discuss the change with others.

- **INTROVERSION** – provide information in writing and opportunity to reflect on the information prior to conversations.

- **SENSING** – provide details of the change (i.e., why, what, when, how, who) and how past change experience is informing this change.

- **INTUITION** – highlight the opportunities the change will present and the future implications of the change.

- **THINKING** – provide the logical rationale (i.e., statistics, research, etc.) for the decision to change, along with the benefits to the organization.

- **FEELING** – highlight the impacts on employees and how the people impacts were considered in the decision making.

- **JUDGING** – provide the plan for how the change will be made.

- **PERCEIVING** – highlight the opportunities to make updates to the plans and the contingency plans in place.

To appeal to all personality types in your communications highlight:

1. **THE BIG PICTURE** – why the change is happening and the opportunities it will bring.

2. **THE DETAILS** – the problems the change will fix and how you came to that conclusion. Also, what is happening, when, how and to whom.

3. **THE NEEDS** – how people will be supported through the change and how the impacts on them will be managed.

4. **THE CRITERIA** – how decisions will be made, the alternatives, and the logical path forward.

Communications also need to:

- **BE TIMELY** – provided to recipients when and as required
- **ANSWER THE 'SO WHAT'** – not just data, but also the impacts, challenges, and opportunities
- **SET THE RIGHT CONTEXT** – make sense in the context of the recipient's role and responsibilities

Consider *who* is communicating and *how*.

During change people like to hear big picture direction and vision from the sponsors (leaders or C-level executives) and be inspired by their words and actions. Then the direct manager is the preferred person to outline how people are personally impacted and what actions are needed. The direct manager is in the best position to motivate people to take action and obtain responses to requests.

It's important that all those communicating set a similar tone within the organization. If all-employee meetings are upbeat and positive, and then meetings with managers and leaders have a doom and gloom tone, there is a conflict in the mood created in the organization. The staff-level employees believe the positive messages but the managers and leaders are hearing different, less positive messages. Balance the mood in communications by being honest and inspirational. Focus on the benefits of the change, outline the effort required to get there and the support that will be provided. Have conversations with your leaders and people managers to ensure they are promoting the same messages.

Lastly, communication planning is about placing information where it will be found. People will seek out information when it's relevant to them, so they need to know where to go when they are ready to know more. I've worked with teams where this meant posting information to the same location each time or posting in multiple locations to ensure that different people could find it. Searching through emails for information when you need it is not ideal. Consider where people go to find things in your organization and

> To get people aligned, make info easy to find.

129

post your information there. This may also be relevant for meetings — instead of hosting extra meetings, build communication about the change into existing meetings and channels. There will still be times when something out of the ordinary is needed to gain attention — an 'all hands on deck' meeting or a special communication letter or release. Take the opportunity to communicate in interesting ways — brainstorm with others and think outside the box!

Communication Tips

1. Provide timely, up-to-date information. Be specific rather than vague, candid rather than guarded.

2. Clearly differentiate between facts, as you know them, and speculation.

3. Stress from change produces selective hearing. Repeat messages frequently and in many forms.

4. Information needs to be perceived as credible. If you don't know, say that. Employees don't expect you to have all the answers, but they do expect you to be honest.

5. Uncover issues. When you know there is a problem or a concern, you can address it. If there is a rumor, you can diffuse it.

6. Make communication easy for leaders. Provide speaking points to help them engage with their teams and stay on message.

The Communication Planning Conversation

Planning and Managing
Conversation 6

PURPOSE

Develop a communication strategy.

WHEN TO HAVE THE CONVERSATION

As soon as you have decided to make changes, then add to your communication strategy as you engage in other planning conversations and find out more information.

WHO'S INVOLVED

- Communication professionals (whoever is in charge of communications in your organization)
- Change leaders to gather ideas and discuss the reasons for specific communication tactics
- Change project team and others with insight into the changes required (e.g., IT for technology changes, HR for people/structure changes, Business Analysts for process changes, leaders and employees with knowledge of the impacted processes, systems, or tools, etc.)

BACKGROUND INFORMATION

Know your current organizational communication channels and statistics on what channels are most frequently used (e.g., newsletter clicks, website hits).

QUESTIONS

- What are the key messages for this change?
- How will we continue to gather feedback from each stakeholder group (see Engagement Conversations for more ideas)?

- How will we know our communication processes are working?
- What rumors are we hearing and how will we respond to them?

The following questions can be listed as columns in a table to develop a communication tracking plan.

- With which audiences do we need to communicate (use your Stakeholder Map as a starting point)?
- What communication tactics will we use (e.g., newsletters, meetings, emails, etc.)?
- What is the purpose of the specific communication tactic?
- What is the frequency of the communication tactic?
- What is the content for each communication tactic (add to this as you go)?
- Who will create the communication?
- Who will deliver the communication?
- What is the status of the communication (e.g., in review, sent)?
- What responses were received from the communication?

NEXT STEPS

- Craft the communication plan, execute, and constantly update the plan based on feedback.
- Download a Communication Plan template at www.actionimpactmovement.com/resources

7. The Performance Conversation

Change means you will need people to do something more, better, or different. Sustaining and maintaining the change means you will need to reinforce the new skills and behavior. The Performance Conversation serves two purposes: (1) to identify the difference between the expected skills and behavior in the current state versus the future state, and (2) to create reinforcement strategies to sustain the new skills and behavior to realize the benefits of the change. This conversation starts with identifying what people will need to know or do to execute the change successfully — do they need to use a new technology platform, behave in a new manner, or follow new processes? You may have captured some of this information in your Stakeholder Conversation. Then you compare what they need to do in the new world with what they do now to find the skill gap. Once you know the skill gap you can decide how to address it. Will people need training? Job aids? Coaching? How will you provide training and coaching? Who will develop job aids? And lastly, how will performance be measured and rewarded to reinforce the new way?

Looking at the following factors, consider what you need to modify or update to create and sustain performance that is aligned to the new expectations:

1. Recruiting and Selection – selecting the right people for the right roles

2. Role Clarity – providing clear role responsibilities and accountabilities

3. Goals – outlining specific priorities

4. Training – offering the right training to build new skills and behaviors

5. Performance Measurement – telling people how they will be measured and aligning measures to the new way

6. Coaching and Feedback – providing the right coaching and feedback at the right time

7. Support – establishing support systems and informing people how to access support

8. Consequences – explaining what's in it for people if they succeed or fail

Gathering input from those impacted is important for this conversation. You need to understand what they do now, what is going to be different for them in the future, and what is going to stay the same.

The Performance Conversation

Planning and Managing Conversation 7

PURPOSE

Identify the knowledge, skills, and behavior gaps between the old way and the new way, then create development plans to close the gaps.

Align performance measures and rewards and recognition programs to reinforce the new structure and expectations.

WHO'S INVOLVED

- HR professionals, change project team and others with insight into the changes required (e.g., IT for technology changes, Business Analysts for process changes, leaders and employees with knowledge of the impacted processes, systems, or tools, etc.)
- Leaders and managers and possibly employees who understand and work in the current state

BACKGROUND INFORMATION

Gather current role descriptions, organizational charts, and performance management information.

QUESTIONS

Skill gap questions

- Due to the change, what do people need to do more, better, or different?
- What current skills will still be required?
- What skills or knowledge will no longer be required (e.g., how to use an old system)?

Role clarity questions

- How are roles changing (e.g., title, reporting line, responsibilities, expectations, behaviors, etc.)?

Measurement questions

- How will we communicate the new expectations?
- What performance measures need to be in place to encourage the new behaviors and skills?
- What information will be provided to help people develop priorities and goals aligned to the new way?
- What changes are needed to align our performance management procedures and documents to the new expectations?
- What consequences will be put in place for success or failure?

Training and performance improvement questions

- When and how will we train people to work and behave in the new way? Who is developing training, job aids, etc.?
- Who will coach people to improve their performance? What is our coaching and feedback model?
- What other support will be made available to people (e.g., champion network, help line, etc.)?
- How will people know how to access support?

Recruiting & Selection questions

- Do we have the right people in the right roles to make this change successfully?
- What do we need to change in our recruiting processes to select the right candidates to achieve and sustain the change (e.g., new role descriptions, recruit from different candidate pools, etc.)?

Reinforcement questions

- Once we have trained people in the new way, how we will continue to help them improve their skills?

- What reinforcement tactics will we need (e.g., on-going training, coaching, performance measures, etc.)? How will we implement them?
- What other people/HR processes need to change to reinforce the changes?

NEXT STEPS

- Revise roles as needed.
- Develop the training and coaching needed to acquire new skills and behaviors.
- Align performance management and recruiting processes to reinforce the new expectations and skills.

8. The Status and Progress Conversation

Project team members will have this conversation the most, *many times with feeling*, during the change effort. Monitoring progress and tasks, making decisions, identifying issues, and capturing next steps are the things project managers live for, or so I'm told!

I'm a fan of keeping things simple, however, depending on the scope of your change initiative you may be in for Gantt charts, project plans, scope documents, issues logs, and decision matrices to keep everything straight. This conversation will happen with different groups of people; for example, the project team will meet regularly to keep tasks on track, then the project leads will meet with the sponsors to highlight progress, address issues, and seek decisions. The structure of your organization and your change initiative will drive who is part of these conversations.

Keep your audience in mind when having this conversation. Sponsors and other leaders generally don't want to know all the nitty gritty details. They want to hear about the progress highlights, the issues and suggested resolutions, and what decisions they need to make. They also want to know any business impacts, and what is being, or needs to be, done about them.

Project teams, those working on the change efforts, need more detail. They need to understand the inter-connectivity of their pieces of the project with others, the deadlines they need to meet, and the decisions that have been made by the leaders. Finding a good flow for these conversations to keep the initiative moving forward is important.

Here's an example of a flow that didn't work! I used to sit through a weekly meeting with multiple project managers discussing multiple projects. Each week the leader started at the top of his list and project managers gave their updates — often the same update each week if it was a slow-moving project. We never made it through the list, yet started at the top again the next week!

The Status and Progress Conversation

Planning and Managing Conversation 8

PURPOSE

Manage the activities, issues, and decisions involved in implementing the change, alter course as needed, and keep key stakeholders informed.

WHEN TO HAVE THE CONVERSATION

All the time!

WHO'S INVOLVED

- The project team for regular updates
- Sponsors and other leaders with the project team for agreed-upon meetings

QUESTIONS

Status and Progress questions

- What decisions are needed?
- What decisions have been made since the last meeting?
- What issues need to be addressed? Who needs to be involved to address the issues?
- What are the risks associated with the change and how are they being mitigated?
- What is the status of upcoming tasks? Are any off track? Delayed?
- What new tasks need to be added to the list?
- Has any new information come to light about the change initiatives?

Stakeholder and communication review questions

- Are there any new activities we need to undertake with our stakeholders?

- What is the status of the communication activities?
- What feedback have we received and is there anything we need to act on?

NEXT STEPS

- Provide status updates to key stakeholders.
- Hold people accountable to complete their tasks.
- Post project information in agreed-upon locations for easy access.

9. The Results Conversation

We can't forget about this one. Did we actually achieve what we set out to do? Look back at your Why Conversation and your What, When, and How Conversation — and ask yourself 'are we there yet?'

Imprinted on my brain, from watching Saturday morning cartoons as a child, is an episode of The Smurfs. On a long journey, the Smurfs constantly ask, "is it much further, Papa Smurf?" to which Papa Smurf patiently responds, "not far now". However, after repeatedly being asked the same question, he finally shouts, "yes it is!". On the path to realizing results and benefits of change it's important to know "is it much further, Papa Smurf?"

Where the Status and Progress Conversation focuses on project deliverables and timelines, this conversation is about the results. Due to the changes we are putting in place — are we winning new customers? Have we realized efficiencies with the new system? Have the customer satisfaction scores increased under the new service methodology?

Revisiting the success questions from the Why Conversation is the starting point. There you defined what success would look like, how you would know when you succeeded, and what indicators and measures were to be tracked.

This regular conversation provides feedback about your change efforts. If you are meeting the desired goals, continue your direction. If you are not meeting your desired goals, determine what course corrections are needed. Input from the Engagement Conversations will be valuable to understand why and how goals are being met or what can be done to get back on track.

Planning and Managing Conversation 9

The Results Conversation

PURPOSE

Assess the outcomes of the change to determine if desired results are being achieved.

WHO'S INVOLVED

Sponsors and other leaders with the project team

QUESTIONS

- What are our success measures?
- What have we achieved?
- What measures and indicators are we tracking?
- What are the current results of those measures and indicators?
- What do the measures and indicators tell us? Are we on track? Off track?
- Based on the current results, what actions are needed?
- What other information is required?
- Who needs to know about results? How will we communicate the results?
- What are we expecting people to do more, better, or different based on the results?

NEXT STEPS

Report results to interested parties — leaders, employees, customers, regulators, external stakeholders and indicate required next steps.

Where to Next?

From here we'll move onto Engagement Conversations. If you're tired of planning and ready to see what people think of your ideas, the next chapter about Engagement Conversations is the place to go. These conversations give you a chance to hear what people think, answer their questions, and build their understanding of the change. While there may be buy-in and support from the senior leaders in the organization, it's often the lower levels that are more impacted by changes — they will spend more time using the new systems or processes, working with the new leaders, etc. Engagement Conversations enable them to travel along their own ABC Transition Roadmap™ to get excited about the change and commit to make it happen.

One More Time with Feeling

Who knew there were so many questions to pose,

Planning is key and this chapter shows,

Where to start to make change and how to keep score,

Now if only we can get all the people on board,

The Engagement Conversations are the way to find out,

If the people buy in or still have some doubts.

Engagement Conversations

9

ENGAGEMENT CONVERSATIONS ARE the must-have conversations to lead change that sticks. These are the conversations you bring to all employees — to the plant floor, the field office, the local branch, and the boardroom — in groups and one-on-one. The change has been planned and announced and now you need to engage people and inspire them to make the change a reality. For change to be successful in an organization, each individual needs to go through their transition from endings, to exploring, to a new beginning. The Engagement Conversations, aligned to the ABC Transition Roadmap™ from Chapter Two, will help people do just that. To prepare to facilitate these conversations, review Chapter Five.

Figure 2.1. **The ABC Transition Roadmap**™

Engagement Conversations	Purpose	Link to ABC Transition Roadmap™
1. The Debrief Conversation	Gauge what people have heard and understood about the announced changes.	Create awareness Build buy-in
2. The Impact Conversation	Identify the impact of changes on people and what they perceive they will lose and/or gain from the change.	Build buy-in
3. The Change Track Record Conversation	Acknowledge the past and identify the actions to bring forward that have worked in past changes and avoid the things that didn't work. Identify the current structure, processes, or activities that will enable the change and those that will hinder the advancement of the change.	Establish belief
4. The Stop, Start, Continue Conversation	Identify priorities to create capacity to implement the change. Create ownership of ideas and solutions to realize the change.	Create capacity
5. The Coaching Conversation	Provide feedback and reflection opportunities to acknowledge and improve on performance needed to execute the change.	Develop capability
6. The Are You on Board? Conversation	Determine a path forward with those people who seem unwilling to change.	Determine commitment to the change
7. The Lessons Learned Conversation	Identify what's working and what's not with the change and adapt as needed.	Continue to learn how to best implement the change
8. The Celebration and Thank You Conversation	Celebrate wins during the change process and thank people for their efforts.	Continue to generate wins to embed the change in the organization

1. The Debrief Conversation

Change happens regularly in organizations and often the folks who've been around for a while think 'this flavor of the month will pass too'. Ouch. Many employees have seen their organization change — new leaders, new technology, new processes — multiple times in their tenure. How will this change be different than ones they've experienced in the past? You will engage them in conversation!

Start with why.

In the Communication Planning Conversation from Chapter Eight we talked about the importance of telling people the reason for the change. Why are we making this change? Why now? What's the risk of not making this change? When big changes are coming — systems, processes, structure — people can feel like their whole world is changing. Communicating why the change is necessary is a great place to start when announcing the planned changes. And as soon as you start communicating what's coming it's time to hold the Debrief Conversation.

The Debrief Conversation assumes the change has been announced — the reason for change, the highlights of what is changing, and perhaps a timeline. This conversation builds common understanding of the why, what, when, where, and who of the announced change. As a leader, knowing how your people are interpreting the change will help you better support them through their transition.

This can be a challenging conversation to facilitate. When change is first announced, there is a lot of uncertainty, and emotions can run high. People interpret information and make assumptions, and the rumor mill can get started right away. Hence the need to have this conversation shortly after the change is announced; to minimize the rumors, provide as many answers as you know, and gain insight into possible resistance in the future. As the change progresses and more information comes to light, you will continue to have versions of this conversation with your teams.

There is a method I often use to facilitate these conversations called the Focused Conversation (from the book *The Art of Focused Conversation* edited by Brian Stanfield for the Canadian Institute of Cultural Affairs, 2000). This approach takes people through a series of questions from objective and reflective questions to interpretive and decisional questions.

Consider who is best to facilitate this conversation. The leader of the group is one option; however, sometimes team members may not be comfortable sharing their thoughts and concerns in front of their leader. If there is reason to believe that team members won't be forthright in front of their leader, consider using a third-party facilitator (internal or external) and meet with the team without the leader. The goal of this conversation is to get people to share their reactions so it's important to create the right environment for this to happen.

The Debrief Conversation

Engagement
Conversation 1

PURPOSE

Gauge what people have heard and understood about the announced changes (e.g., why, what, when, where, who).

WHO'S INVOLVED

- Full team or a group (e.g., all managers across business units)
- The leader of the team or group (if the leader believes the group will be comfortable sharing reactions while they are present)
- Consider a neutral facilitator (internal or external)

QUESTIONS

Objective questions: Focus on facts

- What have you heard or seen about the changes happening in the organization?
- What have you heard people say about the changes?
- What has already changed?
- What facts do we know about this change?

Reflective questions: Focus on feelings and reactions

- What surprised you?
- What did not surprise you (we've seen this done before)?
- What sounded like good news?
- What sounded like bad news?
- Why do you believe we need to make this change in the organization?
- What are you most concerned about at this time?

Interpretive questions: Focus on impact and interpretation

- How will these changes affect our team/organization?
- Which of the changes seem aligned to our current purpose/direction?
- Which of the changes do not seem aligned to our current purpose/direction?
- Who will be most impacted by the changes?

Decisional questions: Focus on action and next steps

- What information do you need to effectively deal with this change?
- What do we need to do differently as a team to move forward?
- What do we need to focus on to move forward?

NEXT STEPS

- Take action on the decisional question responses.
- Follow up with individuals who appear to need more information or support based on their responses in the conversation.

2. The Impact Conversation

Where the Debrief Conversation uncovers what people have heard and seen about the change, and what further information they need, the Impact Conversation focuses on how the changes will personally impact individuals. This may be a group conversation or a series of one-on-one conversations. As we saw in Chapter Three, resistance is inevitable, and as we know from the Seven Dynamics of Change, people focus on what they will lose due to a change before they recognize what they might gain.

The Impact Conversation uncovers people's fears and concerns, which is the starting point for them to start to buy into the change.

The Impact Conversation is about perspectives and perceptions. Holding this conversation will provide insight into the perspectives of your team members. Understanding different perspectives will help you to uncover resistance, find leaders where you didn't expect to, and discover ideas in unusual places. Changing perspectives will enable a successful transition through change.

As an example of perception, when asking the 'loss' questions it's important to let people know that there are no right or wrong answers. What is perceived as a loss is different for each person based on their personal situation (e.g., their role, experience, desires, personality). What some people view as a loss may be viewed as a gain by others. Knowing people's perceptions will help you engage in further conversations as well as craft a strategy to address their concerns.

As you listen to people's responses to the Impact Conversation questions, you'll see leaders emerge — those who may become your champions of the change. You'll also discover who needs more information and why they will resist. This enables you to address resistance early so take note.

When people have a chance to assess the change — the possible losses and gains — and understand their personal impact, they start to buy into the change. They will still need more specific information, training, and coaching to be capable of behaving in a new way and to ultimately commit to the change, but buy-in is a start and the chance to verbalize their fears and be heard is the beginning of buying in.

Engagement Conversation 2

The Impact Conversation

PURPOSE

Identify the impact of changes on people and what they perceive they will lose and/or gain from the change.

WHO'S INVOLVED

- Full team or a group (e.g., all managers across business units) — as a group or in one-on-one conversations
- The leader of the team or group (if the leader believes the group will be comfortable sharing reactions while they are present)
- Consider neutral facilitator (internal or external)

QUESTIONS

Impact questions

- What changes do you think will have the biggest impact on our team, in terms of changes to our processes, structure, governance, technology, or outputs?
- What will you/our team need to do differently to execute on the changes?
- What habits will we need to unlearn to work in the new way?
- What is not changing for us?

Loss questions

- What do you perceive you will lose due to this change? How will that loss impact you?
- What is ending with this change?
- How likely is it, in your view, that the perceived loss will happen?

- What, in your view, could be the worst loss due to this change (personally or for the team)? Why do you feel it's the worst?
- What are we not losing from this change? What is not ending?

Gain questions

- What do you believe you/our team will gain from this change?
- How will the gain impact you/our team?
- What actions are you willing to take to realize the gain?
- What would be the best thing you/our team would like to gain from this change? Why would it be the best?

NEXT STEPS

- Feedback any relevant information to the change project team to include in their stakeholder mapping (e.g., perceived losses to address) and communication planning (e.g., perceived gains to be included in key messaging).
- Follow up with coaching conversations to help people through their feelings of loss.
- Focus on gains during team meetings and one-on-one discussions.

3. The Change Track Record Conversation

Change has happened in your organization before. Talking about what has happened in the past and learning from it through conversation gives you a better chance of not repeating the bad stuff.

When I survey people about their best experience with change some only remember the changes that went badly; these experiences stand out because of the negative emotions etched in their minds. Those with positive experiences speak about the impact of the leaders and the opportunities to help people through the change. Very few mention the system or the process or the business results of the change. Interesting. This will likely happen in your Change Track Record Conversation; people will remember the feelings they had, the struggles they had to overcome, and how the leaders stepped up, or didn't, during the change.

This conversation is the opportunity for your team to reflect on and acknowledge the past. Acknowledging the past and what people need to leave behind is part of the transition process. As I outlined in my 'teeth' story, when the past is not acknowledged or when it is outright dismissed as wrong, people may resist moving to the new beginning. The decisions and actions of the past served the purpose at the time, it's important to acknowledge that before moving on.

When teaching a change management course I used the analogy of a couch I had in university. It was a hand-me-down from other students and served its purpose perfectly during my final year at school. However, with a new job and moving to a new city, the couch was left behind. It wasn't that the couch was no longer useful, it just wasn't going to fit in my tiny new apartment. It was time to let it go! When leading this conversation, I often like to perform the ceremonial ritual of ripping the 'let it go' list off the wall or having each person write down one thing they need to let go of to move forward with the change and place it in a bin in the middle of room (or the trash bin on their computer).

"Silence ensures that history repeats itself.
Erin Gruwell

Reflecting on past change efforts and what worked and didn't work is the chance to avoid repeating history. This conversation is also the opportunity to identify the current structure, processes, or activities that will enable the change to move forward and the obstacles that will hinder the advancement of the change.

Enablers for change may include:

- Involvement of some employees in the change initiatives
- Regular communications and meetings about the change to keep people informed
- Implementing changes that directly address employee feedback and requests

Obstacles to change may include:

- The changes are far away. Momentum may be lost and fatigue of hearing about the change may set in by the time people need to actually do something different
- Cynicism from the baggage of past changes
- Fears and speculation of what may be lost during the change

Engaging in this conversation as a team highlights different perspectives on past changes. Where some people felt a change went well, others may have a different view based on the personal impact of the change. I've seen this conversation bring teams together when they reminisce about shared experiences, often challenging ones, and have emerged stronger on the other side.

The Change Track Record Conversation is also the time when people will, hopefully, start to realize that they have been through many changes before and have learned, gained, and lost, but overall they and their organization are still moving forward. Recognizing their personal ability to overcome the challenges of past changes leads people to the stage of believing that the change is possible on the ABC Transition Roadmap™.

Engagement Conversation 3

The Change Track Record Conversation

PURPOSE

Acknowledge the past and identify the actions to bring forward that have worked in previous changes and avoid the things that didn't work.

Identify the current structure, processes, or activities that will enable the change and those that will hinder the change.

WHO'S INVOLVED

Full team or a group (e.g., all managers across business units)

QUESTIONS

Change track record questions

- Think about the duration of your career at this organization, what changes have happened (i.e., create a timeline of these changes as people list them)?
- What changes did you view positively? Why?
- What changes did you view negatively? Why?
- What practices were in place or what actions were taken that helped the change be successful?
- What practices or actions negatively impacted the change?
- How will we position our team/organization to be open and accepting of changes in the future?
- Why do we think this change will be different (or the same) as past changes?
- If this change means working with different groups, what has been your experience working with that group in the past? Positive? Negative? What perceptions do we need to change?

Acknowledging the past questions

- How do we want to acknowledge and remember the past?
- What might we choose to hold onto from the past? At what cost?
- What do we need to let go of (as a team or as an individual)?

Enablers for change questions

- What structures and processes are in place that will enable the change?
- What skills do we have already that will support the change?
- What activities do we do now that will enable the change?
- What else will enable the success of this change?

Obstacles to change questions

- What structures and processes are in place that will hinder the change?
- What skills are we lacking to execute on the change?
- What activities do we do now that will hinder the change?
- What else will hinder the success of this change?

Next steps questions

- What will we commit to doing differently to enable the success of this change?
- How will we hold ourselves accountable to making it happen?

NEXT STEPS

- Take action on the next steps responses and other actions noted in responses.

4. The Stop, Start, Continue Conversation

One of my favorites! This is the chance to gather useful information from your teams and employees and even customers — involving them in solving problems and creating solutions. I believe that most of the knowledge needed to transform your organization already exists within the minds of your people and your customers. But you need to get it out of their minds, and not by using Jedi mind tricks. You do this by having conversations — you saw that one coming!

Your people know the things they do in a day that add no value and they know the things that they should be doing to make the organization better, but they don't have the time, resources, or authority to do so. Now is your chance to ask them and empower them to make things happen. Making some changes to your day-to-day operations is the opportunity to increase capacity, which will be needed to undertake the change. For example, spending less time running reports that no one reads frees up capacity (time and resources) to learn a new system, or coach a team member, or review the new process document to provide input. This is the perfect conversation to take on the road — to the branch, to the plant, to the field office — to see, hear, and experience the ideas of your people.

When adding new initiatives, you must consider what can be removed or what resources need to be added to complete the extra work.

I realize in this world of 'do more with less' that is a challenge, but it's a challenge that you must accept. Adding more to people's roles won't drive change. Most people already feel that they don't have enough time or resources to complete their current day job so adding new and different activities without taking anything off the to-do list will create more stress. People need a chance to recharge after a busy time before they can take on something new.

You will not have all the answers when leading change and you may be hesitant to open up a 'Pandora's box' of suggestions and questions from your people. However, without providing the opportunity for input you may get compliance to the changes, but not commitment. This is not good in the long run.

In this conversation you will identify projects and operational activities that can be stopped (for a period of time or forever), continued (must continue to happen), or need to be started (new ideas that will make things more effective or efficient). The final must-do for this conversation: follow through and make decisions, don't sit on the fence. Stop the things you said you would, and start the things you promised. Obviously, you need to validate what's possible, but you can't ask for the input if you aren't going to act on it, and don't use that as your excuse not to have the conversations. You also need to be prepared to have some uncomfortable conversations with those whose projects you may need to stop.

People are more likely to support change if they have played a part in creating it.

Landing change on others with no opportunity for input will make the transition longer and more costly. As the old African proverb states: If you want to go fast, go alone. If you want to go far, go together. This works wonders for getting kids to eat their dinner — if they help prepare it, they are more likely to eat it. The same is true in organizations, when people help create change, they have a vested interest in seeing it become successful and encouraging others to do the same.

The Stop, Start, Continue Conversation is fairly straight-forward — what do we want to stop, start, or continue in our business? The key is to then actually do it! Based on the number and type of ideas generated you may wish to rank or prioritize activities through voting or applying specific criteria. You may not be able to follow through all on the suggestions, however, you need to acknowledge the input, tell people what

> If the answers are all your own, you'll be leading the change alone.

will happen next, and follow up regarding actions. Generating the list and never acting on it will damage your credibility as a leader.

Engagement Conversation 4

The Stop, Start, Continue Conversation

PURPOSE

Identify priorities to create capacity to implement the change.

Create ownership of ideas and solutions to realize the change.

WHO'S INVOLVED

Full team or a group (e.g., all managers across business units)

QUESTIONS

Idea generation questions

- What will we stop doing in our team (e.g., activities, processes, tools used, meetings, communications, etc.)?
- What will we continue doing in our team?
- What will we start doing in our team?

Prioritizing, ownership and accountability questions

- What actions are top priority?
- What criteria will we use to rank the priorities (e.g., cost, ease of doing, impact on operations, etc.)? Then rank them.
- By when will we action the stop and start suggestions?
- Who will lead the stop, start, and continue actions?
- How will we know when we have been successful at stopping, starting, and continuing the activities?
- When and how will we follow up on the agreed upon actions?

NEXT STEPS

- Stop, start, or continue what you said you would!

5. The Coaching Conversation

The time has arrived. People now need to do something more, better, or different. But what? Individuals will have many questions on their minds as the change draws nearer.

- How will my job change? Will I still have a job?
- What is my career progression? Who will I report to?
- How will my compensation be impacted? Will I be rewarded differently?
- What are the new expectations and how will I be measured?
- What new skills do I need? How will I gain the new skills?

Many of these questions will be answered during the Performance Conversation from Chapter Eight and then hopefully communicated as decisions are made. Providing the answers to these questions, and other questions people may have, is the first step in this conversation, the second step to set the expectations of what they need to do in the new world and how what they do contributes to the overall purpose and direction. The final step is to coach and provide feedback to enable people to learn, improve, and succeed in the new world. This is definitely a conversation you will have — *one more time with feeling!* I could write another book entirely on coaching — and many people already have — so this will be a much-abridged version of the coaching conversation where we focus on meeting expectations.

You need to set your expectations high — people will generally rise to the level of expectations you set for them — or drop their performance to meet low expectations. So aim high. Yet, don't take for granted that people will know how to do things in the new world. Explain the new way in simple terms. Allow time for practice. Allow time for learning, mistakes, and

> Raise the bar when you need your team to go far.

frustration. Support them with training, job aids, time, and coaching to get better. On-going coaching is one way to reinforce and sustain the changes.

Coaching conversations — along with organized training, changes to role descriptions and rewards programs, and reinforcement tactics — will enable people to build the capability and the resilience to execute the organizational change.

Coaching is an opportunity for people to learn through self-reflection.

This is not the time to be giving advice. As the coach, ask a question then be quiet. Allow people time to self-reflect and respond. You may have your own observations or even advice to give, but let the other person talk first. Remember, this conversation is meant to deepen learning. By providing your advice and observations first, others miss the opportunity to think about what they did well or need to change. Always solving your people's problems will not help them learn so encourage them to take risks. Support your people but don't remove their responsibility.

Lastly, everyone will need coaching during a change, even the leaders. Engage in coaching conversations to build your own resilience and learning as well.

The Coaching Conversation

Engagement
Conversation 5

PURPOSE

Provide feedback and reflection opportunities to acknowledge and improve on performance needed to execute the change.

WHO'S INVOLVED

One-on-one discussions between the leader and team members, or specific coach and coachee, or between peers

QUESTIONS

The following questions assume the expectations have been set and questions regarding role, training, and performance management have been answered.

Coaching for expectations and performance questions

- What questions do you have regarding the new expectations?
- What challenges are you facing right now?
- What opportunities are you facing right now?
- What support do you need to address your challenges or opportunities?
- What will you do next?
- How will I know?
- What did you learn through this conversation?

Simple coaching questions (use to reflect after meetings, projects, or personal interactions). Remember, let the coachee answer first before providing your observations on the same questions.

- What worked well?
- What didn't work?
- What will you do differently next time?

NEXT STEPS

- Continue your coaching conversations, this is definitely a conversation to have *multiple times with feeling.*
- Hold people accountable to the new expectations — including yourself.

6. The Are You on Board? Conversation

The only way for an organization to realize the benefits of change is to have the majority of people on board and embracing the new way of doing things. Notice I say the majority of people. From experience, it's unlikely that you will get 100% of your people to accept the change. So, when is the right time or what are the factors that warrant removing non-committed people? You need to consider how harmful those who are not on board will be to the overall acceptance. Are they in a leadership position? Do they hold a key operational position that will cause a breakdown in a new process? If yes, there may be consideration for removing that person, if possible, or focusing them in an area where they can continue to add value and not inhibit the progress of the change.

Leaders need to be mindful of those not willing to change. Other team members will notice if certain people don't have to change, that their 'non-compliant' behavior is condoned, and they may start to question the leader's efficacy. It may not be feasible to remove people who are unwilling to change, but you do need to be cognizant of the impact of their behavior on the overall implementation success. And, you need to have a conversation — *one more time with feeling* — to help them understand the impact of their behavior and decide on next steps.

Don't circumvent the problem, address it. And don't give up on the person right away, meet them where they are at, uncover why they are resisting, determine what motivates them and encourage them to move forward. This won't work with everyone but it's worth a shot, especially for valuable team members.

Preparing for the Are You on Board? Conversation

People may not realize the impact they are having on others — remember our resistance pyramid — not aware, not able, not willing. You need to check in on the first two before jumping to the conclusion that they are simply not willing. However, if you are at the point of having this conversation then you likely have many examples of behavior that is hindering the change and so you need to prepare to have this conversation.

To prepare for this conversation you need to document the behavior the person is demonstrating and the negative impact of it. Consider the following questions:

1. What are they doing to not comply with or commit to the change? Gather specific examples.

2. What is the impact of their actions on others? On the overall change?

3. What is their contribution to the team/organization? What will be lost if they leave? What is at stake if they stay and continue the same behavior?

4. Why might this person be resisting the change?

5. What are the options for this person if they do not comply or commit?

6. What consequences are you willing and/or able to enforce?

I coached a leader who had a long-time team member who simply would not work in the new way. He ignored requests, refused to engage in required client conversations, and didn't provide useful feedback to his people. The leader had countless conversations with this person to better understand his point of view and demonstrate the negative impact of his behavior on others who were trying to work in the new way. Other team members also raised their concerns about this person's behavior.

The leader knew that the team was looking to him to deal with this person. On a personal level this person was friendly but when it came to work he was fiercely entrenched in the old way and remained immoveable. He was not willing to try the new way, even when offered support, and this unfortunately hampered his destiny. But when the leader escalated the issue, there was no appetite to remove this person. This situation resulted in the long-time team member being refocused on specific tasks and no longer having direct reports. This was the best possible option in the situation and demonstrated to the team that unwilling behavior was not going to be rewarded.

You may find yourself in a similar situation where you cannot change the mind of a dissenter, nor can you remove them, which can be very frustrating. Determine the next best approach, then try to spend less time with this person — because they are usually the ones who suck up a lot of your energy. There are many people who *are* on board with the change and they need your time and support.

As a leader, you've likely felt the sting of not being able to execute on all the things you'd like to do. You can't always *just fire* someone even though everyone thinks that's what should be done. You can't always change policies at the drop of a hat or buy new equipment that is needed. Those not in management or leadership positions don't always understand the give and take challenges that come with being a leader. It can be hard to be seen as a great leader while working within the confines of company policy and procedures. But you need to tackle issues head on, and people issues are at the top of this list.

For most people, engaging in the Are You on Board? Conversation will be one of the most uncomfortable conversations to have. There is a high chance of conflict and most people like to avoid conflict. However, the risk of *not* having this conversation is significant — others see the bad behavior that is allowed and lose faith in the leader to effectively lead. It's also likely that the non-committed person or people are causing you a lot of personal angst — you think about them, you vent your frustration about them, you lose sleep over what to do. Addressing their behavior sooner rather than later is better for everyone.

| Engagement Conversation 6 | The Are You on Board? Conversation |

PURPOSE

Determine a path forward with those people who seem unwilling to change.

WHO'S INVOLVED

One-on-one discussions between the leader and specific team members

QUESTIONS

Review your notes about this person's behavior and impact.

Set the stage as to why you are having the conversation — you want to discuss their commitment to the change and you have feedback to share about their behavior.

Awareness questions

- Are you aware of the reason why the changes are being made? Where do you agree with the reason and where do you disagree?
- Are you aware of what you need to do more, better, or differently to execute the change?
- What have you done to work in the new way?

Reaction questions

- Provide the feedback you have about their behavior.
- What is your reaction to the feedback? Tell me more? What else?

Ability questions

- What support do you need to learn the new way?

Willingness questions

- Are you willing to work in the new way?
- If the answer is no to the above question, ask: What would change your mind to work in the new way?
- When and how will you do things differently?
- What support do you need?

NEXT STEPS

- Based on the responses to these questions you'll have to decide next steps.
- If the person is willing to try the new way, devise a plan with a specific timeframe to complete it.
- If the person is not willing, consider what action is possible based on role options, termination policies, and the appetite of senior leaders to support you in addressing the disruptive behavior.

7. The Lessons Learned Conversation

Did it work? Are we getting results we desired? Pausing to reflect on what's working and what's not and what has been learned during the change effort is another opportunity to engage your team. The key is to implement the lessons learned!

I worked in a manufacturing plant that had compounding issues over the holidays — orders lost, delayed, or partially-filled, staff away, and equipment on the fritz. The leadership and the supervisors gathered to debrief the mess. We documented the lessons learned and developed remediation plans. Over the following months we put new processes in place and equipment was upgraded to avoid a similar situation in the future. Come the following holiday period we revisited the lessons learned and planned accordingly, resulting in a much better and less stressful production run.

Lessons learned should cover a wide range of topics — from what was changed, to how the changes were communicated, how training was done, how performance management was impacted, what resulted from the changes — and identify actions that can be taken during the current change and what should be considered for future changes.

The Lessons Learned Conversation

> **Engagement Conversation 7**

PURPOSE

Identify what's working and what's not with the change and adapt as needed.

WHO'S INVOLVED

Full team or a group (e.g., all managers across business units)

QUESTIONS

- What is working to make this change successful?
- What is hindering this change effort?
- What lessons have we learned during this change? Cover topics such as:
  - Communication
  - Structure
  - Processes
  - Technology
  - Training and coaching
  - Performance management (i.e., rewards, recognition, measurement)
  - Other
- What actions do we need to take now to address the lessons learned?
- What actions do we need to take during future changes?
- How will we hold ourselves accountable for ensuring we act on what we have learned?
- How will we track and manage our actions?

NEXT STEPS

- Keep the lessons learned top of mind — take action on those relevant to the current change and circle back to those relevant to future activities.

171

8. The Celebration and Thank You Conversation

This makes it sound like we're at the end of the change, but as we know change is constant. Your Celebration and Thank You Conversations should be constant as well. They are an important part of encouraging people to continue in the direction of the change and motivate people to want to attempt change again in the future. Generating short term wins is a key tenet of John Kotter's Leading Change model (*Leading Change*, John Kotter, Harvard Business School Press, 1996).

Celebrating those wins and thanking people for their contributions are the conversations that will demonstrate your appreciation and encourage people to continue to generate more wins. Wins may be learning something new, or accomplishing a goal, or achieving expected results. Wins are also seeing progress in the right direction.

Celebrating wins is another way of demonstrating new behaviors. Recognizing the right things — doing work in the new way, using a new system or process, collaborating with new team members, or making decisions in alignment with the new direction — is a way to encourage others to adopt the desired new behaviors. Celebrating is an on-going practice to employ as a leader and not just celebrating individual efforts, but also the efforts of the team.

This conversation can be formal, as part of team meetings with recognition on the agenda, and should also be informal — in the hallway, one-on-one conversations, and in spontaneous situations where the 'thank you' may be unexpected but so appreciated. There are some people who are not comfortable being singled-out, even for praise, in larger groups. Take this into consideration when offering thanks and celebrating wins.

Saying thank you is easy, yet we don't do it enough. And the key is to tell people why you are thanking them.

Saying thank you is like giving feedback — be specific — saying 'great job' doesn't help the person repeat that great job in the future because they aren't sure what part of what they did was great. It feels good to be told 'great job' or 'thank you' but I encourage you to take it one step further — answer the 'for what?' question. Thank people for something specific. "Thank you for staying late to complete the report, having that for the meeting this morning meant I was able to demonstrate our progress to the committee." Or, "Thank you for spending the time to learn the new web platform and helping the team to meet the deadline for posting content." Being specific helps the person recognize how they contributed to a positive outcome.

Engagement Conversation 8

The Celebration and Thank You Conversation

PURPOSE

Celebrate wins during the change process and thank people for their efforts.

WHO'S INVOLVED

Full team or a group (e.g., all managers across business units) or peers to each other

QUESTIONS

The questions for this conversation are more for the 'sender' to consider ahead of time.

Celebration questions

- What has this person/team done that calls for celebration?
- How has what they have done contributed to the success or forward momentum of the team?
- What is the best way to celebrate this win?

Thank you questions

- What has this person/team done that calls for a heart-felt thank you?
- How did they contribute to me, the team, the organization?
- What is the best way to thank this person/team?

NEXT STEPS

- Thank people in the moment where appropriate and possible.
- Keep a log of things to celebrate and thank people for, so things don't get missed.

Where to Next?

If you are here, you are amazing! There is a lot of information in this book. Perhaps this is your first time through the whole book, if yes, keep going you're almost done! On the following pages there is one more great rhyme and there are four ways that I can help you lead change that sticks in your team or organization. Read on!

If you've ended up here because you're referencing the Celebration and Thank You Conversation again, that is also amazing! Thank you for reading this book, I hope it's been a valuable resource on your change journey.

Talking Change — One Last Time with Feeling

"If you are a block ahead of the parade…you're leading it. If you are two blocks ahead of the parade, you aren't even in it.
L. Kratz

AS YOU ENGAGE in your AIM Changing Conversations — *one more time with feeling* — it's important to make sure that your people are actually with you.

It reminds me of walking with my mom. I'm several inches taller than she is and I tend to walk fast. She is often a few steps behind me, sometimes a short city block, and her comment is always, "I feel like I'm walking with the queen". Don't do that, don't be the queen. Be a leader who walks beside their people and guides them through the change.

We have all heard it said that 'people hate change'. But we also know that change is inevitable. You can embrace it and learn from it, or you can fight against it. But it's happening, and successful change doesn't happen *to* people, it happens *with* people — when you're engaged in conversation.

Think of the organizations that no longer exist because they refused to change or didn't change fast enough. Change provides opportunities for learning and growth. In organizations growth is necessary for survival; growth in customer base, growth in knowledge, growth in skills and abilities to react to, or better yet, create new opportunities. When we learn to embrace change, we become better leaders, better employees, and ultimately better organizations.

One Last Time with Feeling

We've hashed it all through, we're all talked out,

We've discussed and debated and figured it out,

Change isn't so bad, when you embrace it with choice,

When each person feels like they've been given a voice,

So go forth and engage, but first plan and prepare,

Not all conversations are easy, some cause more grey hair,

The way forward is clear, to build confidence and lead,

You must converse with others to make change, yes indeed.

Acknowledgements

To my husband, who doesn't always love change, but embraces it anyway, and who makes sure that the things that matter most don't change. You are the rock in our family and the best partner I could have on our hike of life. Thank you for everything you do.

To my two best girls, who make me proud to be their mother.

To my parents, who always encourage me when I've set my mind to something. To my Dad, who passed along his love of organization and paperwork, which served me well in the writing process. To my Mom, who engaged me in countless conversations about work and life from a young age. To my Brother, for his enthusiasm for anything tech and getting me started with my first business website so long ago. And to my Sister, who has listened, cheered, and brainstormed ideas for our next adventure together.

To all the Campbells — as I said in my wedding speech, "they say you marry the whole family, not just the man". I certainly got lucky with my 'gift with purchase', as you are a wonderful family.

To my editor Genevieve Pardoe of Fallon Publishing. Thank you for your patience, your enthusiasm, and of course your great editing and direction.

To Oana Rafaila for bringing my vision to life with her amazing book and cover designs.

Thank you to all those who've been on this writing journey with me — Theresa Lambert, Natalie Sisson, Ali Macintyre, Kallin Moore and all those who provided their valuable input.

To all my colleagues and clients, without you there would be no stories, no experience, no book. Thank you for partnering with me over the years to learn, lead, and succeed. A special mention to Bob Young, who always willingly engaged in a *one more time with feeling* chat with me and to Niki Rankin, who sparked my passion for enabling change — you both left us too soon.

About the Author

JENNIFER CAMPBELL is a seasoned coach, consultant, and facilitator with twenty years of experience leading complex change implementations. Clients seek her out because of her diverse management consulting and leadership coaching background and her ability to create beneficial and sustainable change in people and organizations. Jennifer holds a Bachelor of Commerce (Honours) from Queen's University and is a Certified Professional Co-Active Coach (CPCC) through the Coaches Training Institute.

After living and working in Toronto for two decades, Jen and her family moved to the mountains on the west coast of Canada where she loves to ski and mountain bike.

Are you ready to take AIM? Let's connect.

jen@actionimpactmovement.com
www.actionimpactmovement.com
in. Jennifer Campbell

Appendix A
Conversation Planner

CONVERSATION	
Purpose	
Audience	
Timing	
Size	
Location	
Logistics	
Questions	
Reactions	

Appendix B
Conversation Agenda

Meeting:

Purpose:

Date / Time / Location:

Timing	Topic	Details and Questions	Presenter
9:00 – 9:15	Introduction	• Introduction slide • Poll question — What is your level of awareness of this initiative? Low, medium, high	Sydney Bristow

Appendix C
In Case You Need More Great Questions!

Lead your conversations with questions. The following lists provides more question prompts for various situations.

General Questions

My personal favorites:

- **HELP ME UNDERSTAND.** Not so much a question as an invitation to better understand a point of view. Use it often! This is because when people ask questions about the change (e.g., why) — it's not because they are resisting, it's because they want to understand.
- **TELL ME...** e.g., tell me how I can help you through this or tell me more about your view on that. Similar to help me understand, it's an invitation for the person to continue talking and a chance for you to learn more.

Why, What, and How Questions

- What is the future vision for our organization? What does it mean?
- What does the future vision look like 'on the ground / in the field'?
- How will the changes help achieve the vision?
- What is the logic behind the change?
- What values are driving the change?

- What is it about the (local, national, global, political, competitor, etc.) situation that explains why the change needs to be made?
- Why do we need to respond to this pressure?
- What would happen if nothing were done?
- Do we have a clear vision of what needs to be done based on conversations with others?
- So what? Any data or information you present should also answer the question 'so what?' — So what does this mean? So how do we interpret this?
- Are we creating a sense of urgency or a sense of anxiety?
- What are the benefits of changing?
- If you were a consultant to this organization, what would you change?
- What is changing and what is staying the same?
- How does this change connect with our current business strategy?
  - Does it represent a departure from the strategy?
  - Does it complement the strategy?
- How will the new technology/equipment support our processes?
- How will this change (e.g., new technology, system, process, etc.) make things better, more efficient, or more effective?
- How might we...? Fill in the blank. How might we make this change happen? How might we speed up the implementation?
- How will we ensure this project (change) is not derailed because people are distracted by other projects/priorities?

Personal Change Journey Questions

- What ended?
- What began?
- What conversations did you engage in to move through the transition from endings, to exploring, to the new beginning?
- What were your feelings during the transition period?

- What was most challenging during the transition period?
- What opportunities did the change represent (i.e., what was the compelling reason for the change, what were you hoping was going to be better because of the change, what did you gain)?
- What did you have to let go of to finally accept the change?
- What was in place to support you through the ABC Transition Roadmap™?
  - How did you become aware of the change?
  - What made you buy into the change?
  - What caused you to believe the change was possible?
  - What support was available to ensure you were capable of executing on the change?
  - What was done to ensure you had capacity to execute on the change?
  - What ultimately caused you to commit to the change?
  - What decisions and actions have you taken to continue the direction of the change?

Culture Questions

One of the factors that shapes resistance might be the culture of a group or organization. Consider the following questions as they relate to your current change journey.

- What are the underlying assumptions that need to be challenged to achieve this change?
- What underlying assumptions can serve as a platform to help achieve the desired future vision?
- What current artifacts, behaviors, values and norms are likely to come under attack or be questioned? What are the new ones that will need to emerge?
- What is the one thing you've always done here, yet you don't know why? Is it time to change it?

Sponsorship Questions

- Who initiated this? What is their motivation?
- Do they have the influence and authority to make others take action?
- What is the current level of engagement of the sponsors?
- Do they understand their role in leading the change?

Leader Questions

Leaders want to be able to answer the following questions for their people:
- What will be achieved/delivered?
- When will it be achieved/delivered?
- How will it be achieved/delivered?
- What is negotiable and what is not?
- What support structures are available to help people through the change?
- How will the change impact me/my people?
- How will communication be handled? Frequency? Medium?
- What style of leadership is needed for the future state, and how is it different than the current style?
- How will we encourage the future leadership style?

Impact Questions

- Where do we think impacted groups currently fall in the transition process (ending, exploring, beginning)?
- What new 'language' will people need to learn (e.g., sales language — from sales to relationship management, process language, etc.)?

- What is new for people?
- What's in it for me (WIIFM)?
- How will this impact my sphere of influence?
- Do I need different qualifications to do the same job?
- How will my training time be accounted for (e.g., paid, unpaid, time off, after hours, etc.)?
- What are the options to not changing, not using new technology, etc? What are the consequences?
- What allowances are there for productivity dips due to learning a new process/system?
- What decisions do I need to make?

Resistance Questions

- Where do we expect resistance to occur?
- Which issues do we think will be most inflammatory — for which audience?
- Where will resistance be strongest/weakest?
- How can we best surface and address resistance?
- What do people know about the change now?
- How will we surface resistance to the change early enough to address it?
- How will we respond to resistance to the change early enough to manage it?
- How will we make sure that employee groups most affected by the change aren't overwhelmed?
- Who is resisting and how can I develop a productive relationship with that person?
- What will it cost if the 'old guard' continues to resist the change?

Capability and Capacity Questions

- What specific knowledge, skills, or attitudes are needed to work in the new way?
- Who currently has the necessary knowledge, skills, or attitudes required?
- Of the people who do not have the necessary knowledge, skills, or attitudes, who can be developed?
- How many people will be required to do the necessary work?
- What are the various roles/responsibilities of the employees? How have they changed?
- How will selection decisions be made? By whom? Based on what criteria?
- What change in staff will improve our efficiencies?
- What behavior and attitudes do we need in people to achieve the change?
- How will employees be supported/encouraged to adapt to the new way?
- Who can I call or talk to when I need help?
- How do I contribute? How does my role contribute to the desired results?
- What tools have been provided to managers to help them manage, coach, and support their people to apply the new changes?
- Who will be the subject matter experts?

Commitment Questions

- How will we ensure that people are motivated to change?
- How will we know when people have committed to the change? What will they do more, better, or differently?
- How will we ensure that people do not view the change as optional?
- Are we measuring the right things?

- What can I do to convince you that I'm serious about this change?
- How can we leverage the commitment of enthusiastic stakeholders?
- How will we continue to gather feedback from each stakeholder group?
- What new opportunities are arising because of this change?
- What's the reason you come here every day?
- What has kept you here for more than 10/20/30 years?

Team Questions

- What are the new team goals?
- What's in scope/out of scope going forward?
- What are the individual team member roles?
- What are our priorities?
- How will decisions get made?
- What level of authority do we have?
- How will we ensure that our team functions well during the transition? And in the future state?
- What are we here to do?
- How will we organize ourselves to do it?
- How will we know we've succeeded?
- Who is in charge?
- How will we work through conflicts about information, accountability, etc?
- How will we work across groups?
- What benefits do team members get from the team?
- Who do I struggle to work with effectively and how will I get to know them better to find common ground?

Customer Questions

- How will the level of service be impacted by the changes?
- How will we minimize any adverse impact to customers?
- Are there key customers who may need special attention during this change?
- What needs to be done to help employees feel comfortable in responding to customer questions or concerns about the change?
- How/when do we need to communicate with customers to let them know what to expect due to the change?

Bring AIM Changing Conversations to Your Team or Organization

By now you're either chomping at the bit to get into conversation or thinking, *conversations seem like a good idea, but there's no way I want to facilitate them!* Don't fret, I won't take you to the starting line of change and leave you there to run the marathon all by yourself!

Here is what you do now:

1. **BUY COPIES OF *TALKING CHANGE* FOR YOUR TEAM:** Let's all get on the same page. Literally. Provide the book as background, then start your conversations! Buy bulk copies of this book for your leaders, managers, sponsors, teams, or champions and as a thank you I'll join you on a call to kick off your conversation planning.

2. **HIRE A SEASONED FACILITATOR:** I will partner with you to plan the right conversations, set the right context, and personally facilitate the conversations. Whether it's conversations to engage employees or conversations to align senior leaders, we'll make it happen.

3. **PARTNER WITH AN IMPLEMENTOR COACH:** Do your leaders need support to navigate change successfully? Are they leading a new team or a new mandate? Working one-on-one or with groups, I'll combine my coaching expertise and change management experience to coach your leaders to plan and execute with confidence. Leading change is never a solo endeavor.

4. **PROVIDE TRAINING TO YOUR LEADERS AND EMPLOYEES:** Want to improve your skills to lead change? Wish everyone understood the ins and outs of change and transition? Need to master the art and science of facilitating great conversations? We will customize our leading change programs to meet your specific needs. Options include virtual or in-person training.

LET'S START OUR CONVERSATION!

Send me an email or reach out on LinkedIn to discuss ideas on how I can help you and your organization realize the benefits of change. I look forward to hearing from you.

jen@actionimpactmovement.com

, Jennifer Campbell

NOTES

NOTES

35853810R00122